The Simplicity and Joy of Meditation

by

Stephen R. Daisy, M.A.

DIMENSION BOOKS, INC.
DENVILLE, NEW JERSEY 07834

Published by Dimension Books, Inc.
Denville, New Jersey 07834

Copyright © 1995
ISBN 0-87193-285-7

TABLE OF CONTENTS

Chapter   **Page**

CHAPTER 1

THE SIMPLICITY AND JOY OF MEDITATION

This is not just another "How To" book. If anything, it is a book on how not to do anything at all, yet achieve the goal, because in order to meditate - more accurately speaking, to contemplate - there is nothing you have to do; there is no difficult technique to learn, in fact, no technique at all, no skill to master, and no secret or magical method. Rather, what is necessary is only a simple understanding that meditation, under the appropriate condition, is a natural response of the human nervous system and that condition is simply...effortless silence, just sitting quietly with eyes closed. Therefore, there is nothing that we must learn or be trained to do because success in meditation is not based on what we do but on the fact that we don't have to do anything at all, as anyone can prove to himself by simply adopting this approach.

So meditation, as defined here, is really contemplation because contemplation is simply effortlessly "gazing" within, so to speak, with no mental effort whatsoever. The word "meditation" is used throughout the book instead of "contemplation" because meditation seems to be the more commonly accepted and familiar term used in most of the literature on the subject. Meditation, however, strictly speaking, always involves some fruitful thought to be considered in depth while contemplation requires no particular thought at all.

In a technological society so used to the intrigue of techniques and systems, this methodless method may seem, at first glance, almost too simple to be believed but if you analyze some of the "techniques" commonly suggested in the literature on meditation, you will notice that they all have one thing in common: The meditator is usually asked to do very little. For instance, it doesn't take a great deal of effort to mentally repeat a mantra or a short prayer, or think of a peaceful scene, or just be aware of one's breathing, or mull over some simple thought, image or the color of your "chakra", a technique which actress Shirley McLain has recently made popular. These techniques work not because of their mysterious influence but because their use requires little or no mental effort. But when the meditator just sits, doing nothing at all mentally, just being quiet and receptive, the same result is achieved. That is why meditation methods, for the most part, are neither right nor wrong; they are simply unnecessary.

This parsimonious approach, therefore, may be disappointing to those who love the mystery of a curious or somewhat mystical technique but as William of Ockham once said, "What can be done with less is vainly done with more," a good lesson not only for bloated, government bureaucracies but for easy success in meditation.

To suggest, however, that we can get something out of doing nothing may seem, at first, illogical and unacceptable to the working public brought up on the idea that there's no such thing as a free lunch. It may also seem like a perfect waste of time for someone just sitting with eyes closed, cut off from normal, sensory stimuli. But it is not wasteful nor illogical anymore than taking time out for a nap would be. The physical and mental stillness that we assume when we meditate is simply the necessary condition by which the mind is enabled to transcend to and experience its own inner depth, that is, the Self, whose nature, as Sankara teaches, is bliss.

> Shining is the sun's nature, coolness is the water's; heat, the fire's; so the Self's nature is Being, consciousness, bliss, perpetual spotlessness.[1]

Meditation, therefore, is not a squandering of our valuable time but the experience of absolute peace and joy flowing from the depth of the human spirit.

So, briefly, in order to meditate all you have to do is: 1) sit comfortably, 2) close the eyes, 3) assume a passive attitude for about twenty minutes to a half hour and 4) end the meditation, not abruptly, but easily and slowly. There will be discussion later in the book concerning some practical issues such as posture, timing, the proper attitude toward distractions, ending the meditation properly and so forth. As for the passive attitude, there is also more to be said, but for a quick, preliminary understanding, all it means is that there is no need for the meditator to make any mental effort such as concentrating on one thought to the exclusion of all others - an impossible and needless task - or trying to make the mind a blank - a common misconception - or straining to keep it from wandering - a futile and unnecessary effort. A certain amount of mind wandering is a necessary and inevitable ingredient of meditation. So the fact that the mind may wander should not be a matter of any concern to the meditator. It is not a sign of weakness of mind or inability to concentrate because concentration is unnecessary in meditation.

Contrary to what is commonly believed and taught, it is not imperative to rid the mind of all distractions. All we need do in meditation is to remain as a passive witness, neither struggling to get rid of distractions nor actively encouraging them. We need only to sit and be and then everything is done for us automatically.

This attitude is not one of irresponsibility or the idleness of "Quietism." Rather, it's a responsible and sensible attitude, based on the understanding of the need not to interfere with the natural flow of the mind. It is simply the necessary means by which, according to Psalm 23, we are led like a lamb to the still waters that lie within. Activity during meditation is intrusive. It tends to hinder the inward dive of the mind. If we just let the mind be, however, it will naturally gravitate within as surely as the rain once released must fall.

Meditation, then, is a time for deep rest to mind and spirit but it is not the rest of sleep. It takes place in and as an expansion of the waking state. It is not a trance nor a form of hypnosis nor an altered state of consciousness nor is it a waste of time. Rather, it is a time for drawing deeply on our own spiritual resources for inner strength and support. It is a time for receiving not doing.

Obviously, there is need for activity in life but activity is impossible without rest as it is shallow without meditation. Meditation, therefore, does not detract from action. Rather, it is the proper basis of action because it gives it depth and direction. Meditation expands consciousness, sharpens the intellect and imagination, clears the mind of negative and destructive thoughts so that our actions, based on much clearer, more positive thinking, become significantly more effective and fruitful. Paradoxically, then, by doing nothing we, in effect, improve action.

So meditation is not a retreat from life; it is the stable foundation on which it must be lived. Always at our disposal as an automatic response of the human nervous system, meditation is the supreme gift of nature, the refreshing oasis, the inner garden, the safe and tranquil haven of the mind. It is also the supreme paradox of life because it is a door that opens only if we make no effort to open it.

Meditation, therefore, as defined in this book is a direct and immediate experience without the need of any intervening medium. It is a transcendental experience in which the mind goes beyond its normal limits of objective reality and "tastes" the subjective reality of itself. It's as if the eye of the mind, so to speak, without the use of any mirror, somehow beholds itself or, comparing it to a body of water, it's as if the surface experiences the stillness and peace of the depth. But what does the mind see when it beholds the bliss of itself at the depth level of awareness? Nothing specific, no particular thought or image but rather that inner, boundless horizon of the mind which Sankara refers to as pure consciousness. But it is an experience that the mind, without knowing why or how, finds more enthralling than anything it can think of or imagine. As Plato describes meditation:

> When the mind returns to itself from the confusion of the senses, as it does when it reflects (meditates), it passes into another region of that which is pure and everlasting, immortal and unchanging and feels itself kindred thereto, and its welfare under its own control and at rest from its wanderings being in communion with the unchanging.[2]

That's why there is no effort involved in meditation because you don't have to make the mind concentrate on what fascinates it in the first place. Once it is given the opportunity to be released from the restrictions of normal, mental activity, the attention is naturally drawn to the supreme Reality which lies within. So there is no need to force the attention to do your bidding despite surface distractions. For instance, when you are watching a good movie, you become naturally absorbed and distractions don't matter. If somebody talks or gets up to leave, you are aware of what's happening but it doesn't disturb your infatuation with the movie. Likewise in meditation, though there may be distractions, sometimes superficial, sometimes deep, sometimes many or sometimes only a few, it doesn't matter. The main "feature" so to speak, still holds its grip on the mind, in this case, the main feature being the interior depth of the mind itself, or however you may wish to refer to it, either as the transcendent Self or the Kingdom-of-God-within. But however you believe or care to characterize it, one thing is certain: the sense of profound peace, deep contentment and an all-fulfilling happiness and joy is the frequent and unmistakable experience in meditation (despite surface distractions which may occasionally shade the experience).

Because of its disturbing simplicity, there are bound to be certain apprehensions about this approach to meditation which is what these next few pages will deal with.

To some people, for instance, this totally passive attitude of mind may appear a little peculiar or unnatural. Of course it is not, no more than taking a nap would be. Even so, they would perhaps prefer some kind of thought, phrase or image to mull over during the meditation. This is fine as long as the thought is uncomplicated and simple like repeating the phrase "Our Father", a mantra or whatever. Some degree of mental activity should not be (and is not) a deterrent to the mind's ability to transcend. The meditator, however, should avoid thinking beyond the simplest consideration, like the above example. The mind should not be kept so busy during the meditation that it is prevented from transcending (diving deep within, experiencing the Self).

There is no need, therefore, for deep concentration or, for that matter, any at all, just as there is no need to think in the first place. The mental repetition of the word or phrase, for instance, should be as effortless as whispering, and not even necessarily that. The handling of the concept or the mental image should also be effortless. An effortless thought is like a spontaneous thought. For instance, when we close our eyes without thinking of anything in particular, we may notice how certain thoughts or images, however important or trivial, will pop into mind spontaneously and with no effort. This is the kind of effortlessness that should be used in the mental repetition of the word or phrase or the thinking of the thought. There is no need, as well, for the meditator to feel obliged to allude to the thought or repeat the phrase a certain number of times, if at all. Obviously, it would be foolhardy to try to keep the thought fixed in one's awareness throughout the meditation. As already mentioned, this would be as impossible as it is unnecessary.

If you prefer the word or mantra repetition method, the trick is you don't try to hold onto the word or mantra with a firm grasp. You don't grab it by the wings, so to speak, so it won't fly away. If it flits into your awareness because you remembered you've been forgetting it, then just effortlessly repeat it (mentally), but when the mind wanders and you forget it again, fine. Let the butterfly go. It will go anyway on its own and it will return on its own. You can't help it if the mind wanders. Just don't try to fixate on your object of consideration. Be willing to let it go. Really, there's no need for it in the first place but if you don't want to give up your mantra or word because you believe in its effectiveness or whatever, that's your privilege, but just don't let it become a ball and chain. Just deal with it lightly, or preferably, not at all because you run the risk of fixating on it so that it could become a hindrance not a help.

As for the mind wandering, those who advocate controlling the mind to keep it from moving about during meditation forget one major point: The purpose of meditation (as defined above) is not to focus with great discipline on one thought but to allow the mind to transcend, to expand consciousness itself, not to beat the mind into submission. In Dr. LeShan's book on meditation, his complaint about the so-called undisciplined mind is a classic example of this kind of misunderstanding. He writes:

> The road of meditation is not an easy one. The first shock of surprise comes when we realize how undisciplined our mind really is; how it refuses to do the bidding of our will. After fifteen minutes of attempting only to count our breaths and not be thinking of anything else, we realize that if our bodies were half as unresponsive to our will as our minds are, we would never get across the street alive. We find ourselves thinking of all sorts of other things rather than the simple thing we have just decided to think about.[3]

Any attempt, however, to focus the mind on one thing such as Dr. LeShan suggests can only lead to strain and discouragement. This is not to imply that there is no need for discipline in life. It is only to say that Dr. LeShan's lament is based on a misapplication of the use of discipline. In the face of this kind of inhuman instruction, it would be no wonder that interested novices in meditation would soon lose all incentive to continue the practice except, of course, for those stalwart and stubborn few who won't give up on anything.

Their only hope for success would be if they slowly but surely disregarded the instructions and followed the natural and evolutionary flow of the mind which will not tolerate any attempt on our part to put a leash or stranglehold on it. Try as we might, we cannot bridle this "unbroken horse" as St. Theresa of Avila called it, nor should we have to. The purpose of meditation is to allow the mind a period of profound rest, not to create inner turmoil and tension. Common sense itself tells us how difficult it is to undistractedly concentrate on one thing and one thing alone even for one minute, never mind fifteen. What we have to do, therefore, is to realize that we have no obligation to do anything but let nature take its course. It's in NOT concentrating, NOT trying, NOT asserting ourselves in any way that we succeed in meditation.

Moreover, all that effort to rid the mind of distractions will not only keep it from diving within but will inhibit the healthy release of stress from the nervous system. When the mind wanders during meditation, this is an indication that something good is happening, that is, the beneficial release of tensions. Distractions or daydreams, somewhat akin to dreaming during sleep, are actually the result of the deep rest the meditation provides the nervous system. This explains why at one moment during the meditation the mind could be very much at rest, with little or no thoughts, and, at the next moment, suddenly spring into active day-dreaming. Then it may return from its travels and rest some more only to wander about again a little later. So the entire meditation could be a series of these mental stops and starts. (For beginners, quite often it is).

But rather than to view this phenomenon, like Dr. LeShan or St.Theresa, as an indication of weakness or lack of the power of concentration, we should recognize it for what it is, namely, a healthy, healing process. Just as dreams are a necessary and healthy part of sleep, so also are distractions a healthy and necessary part of meditation because they are an indication of the nervous system actively releasing stress. If our dream-sleep is somehow interfered with, we miss out on the full benefit of a night's sleep. But if we try to block distractions during meditation, it's like trying to block a natural process. Meditations, therefore, which are sometimes restless and full of uncontrollable distractions are simply an indication that the nervous system is sloughing off a lot of stress.

But the amount of stress released varies from one meditation to another, for reasons not yet understood, thus partly explaining why some meditations are seemingly more restful and consoling than others. Both types of experiences, however, are equally valuable. Though they may seem like contradictory phenomena, they are, in fact, intimately connected in a cause-and-effect relationship because the deep rest of the meditation actually causes the mind to wander from time to time just as deep sleep causes occasional dreaming during the night. As the nervous system unwinds because of the profound rest, as the knots of stress are loosened, the activity of this process stimulates the imagination and a day-dream is born, the mind wanders, and the feeling of sweet repose, though not wholly lost, is somewhat overshadowed.

Sometimes also a meditation may seem completely without distractions and feelings of restlessness but the next one following could be filled with churning thoughts and images. This is because the deep rest of the previous meditation led to the release of stress in the one following. A previous one, in other words can influence the course of the next.

But we should not be discouraged by these unpredictable swings of mood and feeling. They are simply the moving light and shadow of an ever-changing picture of spiritual growth. Rather, we should regard them with the same acceptance and trust as we do the shifting patterns of the weather. Though we do not fully understand its unpredictable character, we know there is an ecologically useful purpose behind its inscrutable behavior. Certainly, we owe ourselves and the inner workings of our own minds and hearts no less confidence. The mind is not an unbroken horse but is more like a stream which, if allowed to flow, will seek its own serene level.

But even if you don't completely accept the stress-release theory concerning mental distractions during meditation, the bottom line is this: Any attempt to try to control the mind from wandering will, because of all the effort involved, tend to prevent the mind from transcending.

In meditation, therefore, the mind wanders as the result of stress being released from the nervous system but there is also the opposite experience in which the mind takes a rest from its wanderings and comes to a serene halt, either for a lengthy or short period of time. And just as it is difficult to keep it from wandering, it is also difficult, when it falls into this state of deep repose, to stimulate it into thinking, imagining, remembering or whatever (not that you would want to). In this state of sweet tranquillity, thinking becomes like an unwelcome intrusion (as well as outside distractions) almost as if, in its deep contentment, the mind had no need to be concerned with objective reality. The faculties seem as if they are asleep, as if lulled by a stronger, internal sense of surpassing sweetness. This is called the "ligature" (binding) of the mental faculties, a term coined by Bossuet, the renowned Catholic theologian of seventeenth-century France.

Yet this condition of mind should not be confused with torpor, lassitude or trance. Though deeply absorbed, the mind is still alert but simply not interested in moving. In this state, it has advanced beyond the level of thinking to the source of thought itself, the very "ground of one's being", as Meister Eckhart terms it, or as Plato described it when he referred to ".. that region of the mind which is pure and everlasting, immortal and unchanging," or, in a religious sense, the kingdom of God that lies within. In this situation, momentarily, at least, thinking or imagining holds no fascination for the mind, drawn, as it is, to the bliss of the inner silence, the splendid void of the unbounded Self. It is similar to when the mind, absorbed in one thought, naturally tends to exclude other thoughts. In this case, however, it is absorbed in the supreme Good that lies within and, therefore, loses interest in thinking altogether during the meditation.

None of the above implies that the meditator could lose control of his own mind. Obviously, he can come out of the meditation any time he chooses. The meditator, remember, is simply permitting all this to happen but this letting go will not lead to any possible loss of control. Meditation is not a trance-like state, though it may seem so to an observer, nor a loss or even a reduction of consciousness. On the contrary, opening up our awareness to the preconscious depth of the mind means, in fact, the expansion of consciousness, not a reduction. Furthermore, the passive attitude recommended for meditation is simply a neutral position not the loss of command. It could perhaps be compared to a man rowing a boat, who having decided to rest, pulls in the oars and drifts for a while. But this is not a case of surrendering control because he has the ability to pick up the oars at any time and continue in any direction he chooses. Of course, the analogy is not perfect because the boat would just drift aimlessly; but in meditation the drifting of the mind, so to speak, is never aimless because it is always toward the peaceful harbor, the still waters of the contemplation. This is the mind's natural tendency.

You could also compare a meditator to a person attending the theater. He or she is there in a passive role as a quiet, appreciative witness of what takes place, not obviously, to direct the play. As these analogies should make clear, the most basic principle of successful meditation is that the meditator should not have to make any effort but be passive, receptive and take it as it comes.

But this experience of deep rest alternating with spurts of mental activity during the meditation is also explained by the fact that these two states, representing two autonomous but opposite functions of the nervous system, tend to somewhat inhibit each other. For example, when the mind begins to wander, then the feeling of sweet repose is partially obscured. But when the mind transcends, the mental faculties seem "bound" (the ligature). So in the early stages of meditation, there is a physiological juggling act, so to speak, going on within the nervous system, as it swings back and forth between these two opposite levels of functioning. As the renowned teacher of meditation, Maharishi Mahesh Yogi, so excellently explains in his commentaries on the Bhagavad-Gita:

> In the early stages of the practice of transcendental meditation, these two levels of function in the nervous system are unable to occur at the same time; the function of the one inhibits the function of the other. That is why, at this stage, either transcendental consciousness or the waking state of consciousness is experienced.[4]

It's probably more accurate to say, though this is just a hypothesis, that meditation in the early stages is not a pendulum-swing back and forth between the two states as if the one were alternately canceling out the other. Rather, as one's experience may prove, it's a question of one state merely predominating over the other, not canceling it. For instance, even during the most absorbing rapture, in which normal mental activity is sharply inhibited, some small amount of it is still possible such as, for example, the power of decision to stop the meditation when one so chooses.

Conversely, a meditator may seem quite relaxed and peaceful to the casual observer but, to the meditator himself, the meditation at that point may seem restless and full of distractions. In other words, he or she can experience a paradoxical state in which the mind seems restless even though the nervous system is deeply resting. This would be similar to the phenomenon of dream-sleep which is considered by sleep researchers as a paradoxical state during which a person seems to be profoundly asleep but shows, nevertheless, certain signs of being awake such as rapid eye-movements (REM sleep), increased heart-rate, brain-wave activity similar to the waking state, and so forth.

In time, however, this see-saw phase in meditation will cease and the two levels of consciousness will be clearly experienced simultaneously in the waking state, but this will only come about gradually and in time through the regular practice of meditation. Again, quoting the Maharishi:

> Now for transcendental consciousness to become permanent and to co-exist with the waking state of consciousness, it is necessary that the two states of the nervous system corresponding to these two states of consciousness should co-exist. This is brought about by

the mind gaining alternately transcendental consciousness and the waking state of consciousness, passing from one to the other.

This gradual and systematic culture of the physical nervous system creates a physiological situation in which the two states of consciousness exist together simultaneously.[5]

So there are two factors involved in meditation: 1) the healing (stress-release) factor and 2) the growth factor. Meditation is not just a question of deep relaxation and the release of stress but the gradual development of a more expanded state of consciousness as the transcendent state and the waking state, initially experienced more or less separately, gradually merge over a period of time and begin to function in blessed unison.

From time to time, however, even in the early stages of meditation, there may be momentary experiences of these two states functioning together harmoniously. This is a most liberating and joyful experience in which the mind seems very active and creative, thoughts spontaneously flowing, along with a feeling of profound peace and happiness. The mind's activity in this state during the meditation is not so much aimless wandering in the release of stress but light and buoyant, surging with creative impulse. During this spirited and blessed state everything seems so hopeful. Perhaps the solution to a long-standing problem may suddenly spring to mind (although it is always wise to reevaluate after the meditation any inspiration that comes during it), or the meditator, inwardly smiling, may feel like singing or laughing. There is also no telling how long this expanded state may last, a few moments, throughout the entire meditation or even sustained for a day or two even in the midst of daily routine, but it will pass, not, of course, without some understandable feelings of regret. Yet this feeling of loss should, in fact, give one reason to be encouraged rather than disappointed because this temporary infusion of great bliss is a foretaste of what life will be like when the nervous system, strengthened and refined by the daily practice of meditation, will be able to maintain this serene, loving and joyful state at all times.

A successful meditation is not just when the mind is a blissful blank as is commonly believed. The feeling of sweet repose is only a part of the meditation picture. As explained above, the mind must wander from time to time either in the release of stress or to function at a more expanded level. It would be a mistake, therefore, for a meditator to become discouraged if a relatively distraction-free experience of bliss is not a regular occurrence nor should he regard it as an end in itself. Though it occurs with varying intensity often enough, it represents only one phase of an on-going process of development in the evolution of consciousness. Ecstasy, therefore, uncoordinated with the normal waking state, cannot be a goal in itself. True ecstasy is when both feet, so to speak, are on the ground, when the mind is in bliss but still anchored in objective reality. There is no such thing, therefore, as an unsuccessful meditation because each one, no matter what its characteristics, be it sweet or dry, rapturous or restless, is an essential element of the on-going alchemy of inner transformation.

In regards to the word "dry" just used, the experience of "dryness" in meditation, in its most strict definition, describes a state in which there seems to be little or no sense of affect at all. This is likely the result of strong stress-release but, as will be explained shortly, this condition is not without its obvious advantages, but one should not make the mistake of thinking that because a meditation is neither ecstatic nor euphoric it is, therefore, dry. The state of bliss seems neither categorically dry nor necessarily euphoric. When the transcendent tends to dominate awareness and mental faculties are partially subdued, the usual result is a feeling of ecstasy. But when the mind starts to become active either as the result of the release of stress or whatever, it tends to temper this feeling, as one's own experience in meditation will prove. One could, therefore, mistakenly regard this felt contrast or come down as "dryness" when, in fact, it seems to approximate a more balanced blend of joy and calm.

So the state of "bliss-consciousness," describing a greater integration between the waking state and the transcendent, seems likely not one extreme nor the other; rather, it seems neither too sweet nor too dry, neither too high nor too low, more an endearing smile than a hearty laugh or more the warm glow of the full moon rising than the glare of the noon-day sun. This may explain why the many ecstasies which St. Theresa of Avila experienced in the early stages of her career were absent in her later life when, presumably, she achieved true serenity of spirit. But this gentle, sweet equilibrium, or aptly coined by Maharishi Mahesh Yogi as "restful alertness," perhaps more profoundly defines what is meant by "bliss-consciousness" or in religious terms, "living in the presence of God" who is described in the Old Testament as "light as a rustling breeze." (Job, 4:12-17)

Every meditation is always a positive and reinforcing experience. Even the so-called restless meditations, which may seem to be the very antithesis of what we would think meditation should be like at all times, are never subjectively without some measure of pleasantness and relaxation though it may not seem immediately obvious. Objectively, and this can't be emphasized enough, body and mind are always deeply relaxed during meditation though we may not always be fully aware of it, (however contradictory this may sound). The proof of this is usually seen right after a meditation of restlessness and strenuous stress-release, the immediate effect being a noticeable feeling of lightness, buoyancy and greater clarity of mind as if a burden had been lifted.

This can be noticed most dramatically in the case, for instance, of an individual suffering considerable distress over, say, some especially upsetting event in his or her life. Though meditation will never allow us to escape reality or make our problems suddenly disappear, it will significantly improve our ability to deal with them in a more detached and positive way. It broadens our perspective and removes the burdensome consequences of anxiety, anger or hostility which a given problem may arouse. In fact, after twenty minutes or so of meditation, the reality of a particular problem may still remain but its unsettling impact on one's peace of mind will be largely gone, which means, in one sense, it's no longer a problem.

This is not to imply that meditation is like an anesthetic for our feelings. It is not an escape from life. On the contrary, it has the effect of deepening our feelings, not dulling them, because it gives us the strength and serenity of mind to dare face them and the real world as well. Of course, complete mastery over our emotions is hardly an overnight achievement but each meditation we make is a significant step in that direction. And that will be the time when the mind will remain, like a windless flame within, undisturbed throughout all crises though every human emotion can be fully felt.

Some people can put on the mask of calm in the midst of crisis even though they are churning from within. The enlightened man, however, need not pretend. His generally peaceful exterior is a genuine reflection of his inner state.

Enlightenment, therefore, does not mean the absence of emotion. It means that one in this state can feel emotion fully and deeply yet not be overwhelmed.

Moreover, the serenity of meditation does not result in false complacency or weakness nor does it dilute a justifiable sense of outrage in the face of injustice. On the contrary, it tends to uplift anger into a more creative impulse for more useful and beneficial purposes. Far from dulling our sense of injustice, it sharpens it. At the same time, it supplants the desire for revenge with the strength to do something about a given grievance in a positive way, avoiding the extremes of either cowardly retreat or violent aggression. Meditation then gives us the ability, eventually, to deal with our anger in serenity.

Perhaps some people may harbor some hidden anxiety about facing themselves in the solitude of meditation but there should be nothing to fear about sitting quietly by one's self. As Thomas Merton, the Trappist monk, commented in his book "Love and Living":

> If we are afraid of being alone, afraid of silence, it is perhaps because of our most secret despair of inner reconciliation. If we have no hope of being at peace with ourselves in our own personal loneliness and silence, we will never be able to face ourselves at all; we will keep running and never stop.[6]

But there is nothing to fear as the very first week of meditating, if not the very first day, will prove. Why should the experience of one's own, deepest being be distasteful? Does the inner Self have a bitter taste? The answer is obvious: Consciousness, as your own experience will prove, at the depth level of the mind is by its very nature peaceful, joyful and loving. Like the bottom of a pond or a lake, the depth of the mind is serene, transcending all the relative joys, sorrows and restless waves of the surface of life. And in time, through the regular practice of meditation, this hidden treasure will be permanently ours to support us at all times in our daily lives.

This means the full expansion of consciousness and a sense of fulfillment and lasting happiness in life. In New Testament terms, it could mean the realization of what Christians pray for in the "Our Father", namely, the kingdom of God on earth, (heaven being considered a state of mind not a particular place). What then is there to fear?

Then there are those who, though they may not have any anxieties about meditating alone, do not have a clear understanding of the sublime purpose and importance of daily meditation. Some people, for instance, meditate only on certain occasions as when the mood strikes them or to ward off a headache, prepare for an exam, or soothe frayed nerves after a particularly difficult day and so forth. Others may have slightly more important reasons such as to reduce blood pressure, improve athletic ability, lose weight and the like. These people recognize the short-term benefits of meditation but, unfortunately, fail to recognize its long term ones. They will then stay with their meditation as long as these secondary goals remain important but once they are achieved, many stop meditating. Meditation is healthful, that is true, but more importantly it leads to the fulfillment of life, to the transcendent joy and happiness which is the destiny of man. Until this goal is achieved, we should never stop meditating.

In summary, meditation as defined in this book is really contemplation because in meditation, strictly speaking, there is always some profitable thought to be considered, focused on and mulled over at length. In contrast, contemplation requires no particular thought except the thought, obviously, that there is no need to have one.

In religious meditation, a person could meditate on some religious verse or a simple word such as "Father" from the prayer, the "Our Father." Reflecting on the idea of God as a loving Father, the meditator is consoled and encouraged by this deeply moving consideration. In contemplation, however, according to traditional teaching on the subject, the mind is not concerned with thinking <u>about</u> God in the abstract but, somehow, actually <u>experiencing</u> Him deep within the Self, the core of one's being, the effect being an all-fulfilling sense of peace, joy and love. In this kind of sapiential, intuitive, non-factual kind of knowledge, the human soul, so to speak, touches or "tastes" the Holy Spirit (St.Bernard) or is "embraced" by Him (St. Theresa of Avila). The difference between meditation and contemplation, then, is like the difference between the mental image of something and the thing itself, like the difference, for example, between thinking about eating an apple and actually biting into it.

Atheists, however, will, of course, explain the experience in their own way. In fact, it makes no difference how one may choose to explain it. The main point is that one should enjoy contemplation on a daily basis, taking full advantage of all its benefits to mind and body.

But even believers would find the notion difficult, that is, that God can somehow be directly experienced. Most people look upon contemplation as something reserved only for those far advanced in the spiritual life, an idea which many spiritual writers down through the centuries have promoted. As for "seeing" God, that's reserved, supposedly, for the after life, according to the teachings of most, major religions as if God were too high in heaven for our fragile, earth-bound humanity. But this teaching originates mostly from certain religious authors and preachers who exaggerate "the God experience", or what it means "to know" God. He is usually pictured as a blinding sun, a vast ocean or an angry Father who must be appeased from His high throne in Heaven. They don't portray Him, as he is described in the Old Testament, as "gentle air" (3 Kings,19: 11-13) or as a "still voice" (Job, Chap.4:17) or as a "shepherd" in Psalm 23, images which more accurately represent the sense of the contemplative or "God experience." It's a teaching which seems to suggest that, as much as man, within his limited capacity, is able to comprehend an infinite God, it is not the experience of looking into a blinding sun. On the contrary, God, in this scenario, is seen as the gentle basis of our humanity, a refreshing breeze (or kindly light) which anyone can experience by simply going within himself and breathing in that divinely gentle air, or "holy spirit" (or "breath," its root meaning) of absolute joy, love and freedom from fear, which is the ultimate fulfillment of life.

All of which is said not to promote religious converts but to help explain the phenomenon. In a sense, religion is really a language man uses to explain his own human experience of transcendence. What is important is not the language but the experience. But in neutral terms, contemplation may be described as the mind simply gazing within to the deepest regions of consciousness, reaching beyond thought to the very well-spring of thought, to the very core of one's being, to the supreme Goodness that lies within.

The way, therefore, to transcendence and total fulfillment in life or in religious terms, the way to heaven, is direct and simple. There is no steep staircase we must climb or a rugged mountain path. Heaven is not far away. It is already here. We simply don't know it. It is not a place where we go after death (whether you believe in life after death or not). It's not even a place. It's life itself and a state of mind. It simply means the full growth, the full bloom of human perception, sensitivity and awareness, gradually evolved through the regular practice of contemplation, or, as defined in this book, meditation. It's a kind of perception that results in a reverential awe, love and respect for people, for our fellow animals and for the planet itself, an awareness the lack of which is the basic cause of the pollution, the misery and sickness which our utilitarian, unfeeling, technological age has brought upon us, and which has spawned the arrogance of the industrial revolution, turning our blue planet into a commodity, a resource to be used at any cost, even if it involves the contamination of the very air we breathe and water we drink, the rape of the land, the destruction of forests, the selfish and brutal reduction of animal habitat, the indiscriminate slaughter of helpless animals, the massacre of our youth in incessant wars, the enslavement and exploitation of people, the blasphemies of industrial noise, filth, corruption, greed and ugliness....all because the world is not regarded as a heaven but as a workplace and dumping-ground, a wilderness to be conquered, not revered and loved.

But to return to the main point, meditating is as easy as breathing. We don't learn to breathe; we just breathe. Breathing takes place as long as there is air and the organism is alive. That is the only condition. So also with meditation: As long as the simple condition is met, that is, just sitting quietly with eyes closed and not making any mental effort, the mind automatically transcends.

Again, for those who enjoy discussing contemplation in religious terms, you could say that we can breathe the divine atmosphere that lies within us just as easily as we can breathe the physical atmosphere that lies without. No effort is required. The Godhead within each person is within easy and direct reach. As Christ said, "Why, then, if you, evil as you are, know well enough how to give to your children what is good for them, is not your Father much more ready to give from heaven his holy Spirit to those who ask Him," (Luke 11,11-14). Again, he said, "Knock and it shall be opened unto you, seek and you shall find." (Luke 11, 9-10) Also: "The kingdom of God is within you." No effort is required to find it. You just knock and the door opens to the heaven that lies within you.

Contrary to what some religions may teach, God is natural to man as your own experience in contemplation will prove. Man is born, so to speak, with the spiritual lungs to breathe in the bliss of the divine. So, in a sense, "spiritual breathing" takes place when a person, just sitting quietly, allows his physical breathing, in the serenity of the meditation, to diminish, which, of course, takes place naturally without any trying. All we have to do is take time out to allow it to happen.

Working people are often too busy nowadays making a living to take time out for a mental "breather." They can be hardly blamed. When they get up in the morning, they have barely time to eat breakfast, get themselves ready for work and their children ready for school, never mind take time out for a few, quiet moments. We are all in bondage to a system which makes it so difficult for us just to survive, the sad casualties of the work ethic, of the Puritanism of the industrial revolution which regards just sitting and apparently doing nothing as a waste of time. But the time has come for all of us either to find time each day for ourselves or remove ourselves from the system as best we can. Maybe it's time for another revolution, for the basic right of all of us to have enough time for our spirits simply to breathe. So, to review briefly the "technique" of meditation, there is none....unless you define doing nothing a technique. All you have to do is sit comfortably, not recline, but sit, close the eyes and basically do nothing, just remain passive for about fifteen minutes to half an hour, and when you decide to end your meditation, you should not come out abruptly. It's not more complicated than that.

So, in summary, in order to meditate, or, really, to contemplate,

YOU NEITHER AFFIRM NOR DENY,

YOU NEITHER FOCUS ON ONE PARTICULAR THOUGHT, NOR TRY TO MAKE THE MIND A BLANK.

NOR DO YOU TRY TO CONTROL THE MIND FROM WANDERING WHEN IT DOES SO SPONTANEOUSLY.

THIS IS A SIGN THAT STRESS IS BEING RELEASED, SOME HEALING TRANSFORMATION WITHIN IS TAKING PLACE, SOME BURDEN BEING RELIEVED AND THE SPIRIT REFRESHED.

YOUR ONLY THOUGHT IS THAT YOU DON'T HAVE TO DO ANYTHING.

YOU ARE LIKE AN AUTUMN LEAF ON THE POND; YOU JUST FLOAT.

YOU ARE LIKE A CHILD BEING GATHERED UP AND CARRIED IN YOUR FATHER'S ARMS. YOU JUST TRUST AND BE GLAD.

YOU ARE LIKE A LAMB BEING LED TO THE STILL WATERS. EVERYTHING IS DONE FOR YOU AND YOU LACK FOR NOTHING.

CHAPTER 2

THE BENEFITS OF MEDITATION

We already understand the main benefit of meditation which is evident most of the time we meditate, namely, the experience of transcending, which in time through the regular practice of meditation becomes a permanent feature of consciousness. To some, however, this concept may seem too abstract or remote. So perhaps it may be helpful to discuss in more concrete terms the significance of this inner experience in the development of consciousness and its effect on one's sense of well-being, attitude and behavior.

First of all, in plainer terms, you could say that meditation leads to one's full development as a human being, which means precisely what? It implies, at the very least, the full bloom of life, a relaxed, healthy body, a mind sharp and clear with a profound responsiveness to and deep appreciation of life. It means the gradual but inevitable rise to the highest level of human consciousness which the ancients express in more dramatic terms such as samadhi, nirvana, satori and so forth, all of which means: Freedom from all sense of suffering, and an awareness of total harmony with one's self and with the outside world. More importantly, it means an abiding sense of love, as if one were embraced by the universe.

In this state, there can never be any feeling of being lost or forgotten even when everything else seems hopeless. This spiritual sense of being deeply loved, and therefore secure and joyful at the very depth of one's being, is the state of perfect freedom in which behavior is based primarily on love, deeply felt and spontaneously expressed. The only disadvantage with these claims is that they seem too good to be true. The truth of life, ironically, almost seems to undermine itself because we are so accustomed to the idea that life must be a continual struggle. This is precisely the problem but, as consciousness gradually evolves to this higher level, the truth of this initially unbelievable revelation, begins to unfold within the framework of one's own personal experience. This is the only proof possible.

In America, we are all really from Missouri. When something sounds too good, we tend to find it suspect immediately, pie-in-the-sky not being a common feature in the philosophy of a highly business-oriented, pragmatic civilization. Perhaps, then, it would be better to state the claims in less dramatic terms like the following: By the regular practice of meditation, we can become more happy and serene in life. Our outlook gets brighter. Our ability to cope with life continually improves. We become less fearful and worried about things, leaving more room for the positive rather than the negative, more room for laughter, creativity and compassion. We become more outgoing and less grasping, more sympathetic with the needs of others and less obsessed with our own. The "windows" of our perception become increasingly cleaner and more transparent. We become more and more in touch with our own feelings and less and less afraid to face them and come to terms with them.

Finally, an inner sense of joy radiates continually from within, a joy that does not depend for its sustenance on the external circumstances of our lives, such as whether we are rich or poor, famous or unknown, married or single, handicapped or healthy. Whatever our situation may be, it basically doesn't matter as long as we ourselves are happy in our own right, fully in touch with the Self whose nature, as Sankara tells us, is bliss.

True human happiness, therefore, is based on the inner life of the spirit, but it doesn't follow from this that we end up detached or disinterested in the world. The opposite is true. It's because of the strength of this inner life that we are better able to enjoy what's happening on the surface of life. And because of this spirit of detachment, which that inner stability provides, we don't lose our perspective in life's ups and downs. We can enjoy our friends, for instance, but not let their slights (real or imagined) disturb our inner peace, at least, not for long. When friendships or loved ones fail us, we take the hurt with greater resignation and serenity of mind. We are not so easily crushed nor so slow to recover from the deep disappointment of love lost.

In fact, this more detached frame or mind of the mellowed meditator is an important ingredient of a success-ful relationship since he (or she) has little room in life for jealousy or possessiveness. It is also the true basis for an excellent sense of humor because it is impossible on this level of consciousness for anyone to take anything too seriously without at the same time being cynical or irreverent.

The skeptics, who try to play down the importance of meditation, by saying it's nothing but this or nothing but that, sadly miss the big picture. The "nothing buters" who may say, for instance, that meditation is just a fancy name for taking a nap or soaking in a warm bath, have simply closed their minds to the idea that there may be something new in life for them to learn. Since the beginning of recorded history, meditation has played a valued part in all the major civilizations of the world both East and West. So the millenia-old claims of the benefits of meditation (the contemplative way or the mystical experience) are altogether too important for a snap judgment or quick dismissal. It's difficult to penetrate this kind of ignorant skepticism which would smugly disregard the culture and traditions of most of mankind down through the centuries. There are none so blind as the blind who claim they can see.

The history of meditation from its earliest origins in Pre-Aryan times of the second millenium up to the present can hardly be the aim and scope of this book. But it would be worth the reader's while to read, at least, a good summary of the history which you can easily find in the reference section of your local library. Look up "Mysticism, the History of," in the Encyclopedia of Philosophy. Written in easily under-standable prose by the renowned theologian, Ninian Smart, it will take you about a half an hour to read and although you won't be deserving of a Master's degree after completing your reading assignment, you will have, at least, some idea of the importance of meditation in the history of mankind.

Reading this article, you will also note that meditation did not evolve just in a theistic, religious milieu, which points up the simple fact that you don't have to believe in God to get the benefits from meditation. Followers of Buddha have been meditating for centuries but outside any religious context, and presumably, profiting a great deal from the practice. The language of Buddhism's more philosophical approach may seem abstract and even impersonal as com-pared, for instance, to the typical fervor of religious ritual and sentiment but it is difficult to see how Buddha's aim in life was essentially different from the great religious mystics of the ages such as Christ or Muhammad.

Buddha talked about the Absolute or the "void" and the need for man to be in contact with the transcendent field of his innermost being while religion has traditionally emphasized man's personal relationship and union with his God. The former is more humanist, the latter more theological but, in reality, the difference between the two is merely semantic. Whether one refers to the Absolute Self in philosophical language or to the Godhead in theological language, the reality remains the same, whatever the name one chooses to give it.

Meditation, therefore, can be practiced both by religious and skeptics alike, satisfying both the religious yearnings of the devout as well as the purely humanist goals of the atheist. Religious who may be shocked by this statement should realize that, in the Old Testament, God is quoted as defining Himself as pure, nameless Existence when he said to Moses, "I am Who am." He has no name. With this definition of God, it's difficult to see any difference between Buddha's Absolute and the nameless Being of the Old Testament.

But if the devotee of doubt disavows even the concept of an Absolute, what is left for this kind of skeptic is the fact of his own personal experience in meditation and its beneficial effects on his own mind and heart. What we believe, therefore, about meditation is unimportant. What is important is the realization that our life is enriched because of it and too difficult to bear without it. Statements by religious that God will not come to a meditating atheist put a limit on God's goodness Who Himself, from what the Bible tells us, is not interested in belief in names. The mystical experience of meditation, therefore, is not the exclusive property of religious groups since poets rhapsodize about it, philosophers analyze it and scientists try to show its physiological effects in scientific journals. Meditation has many tongues and a vast variety of terminologies. The student of meditation, no matter what his background, can, therefore, benefit greatly by approaching the subject from many angles, thereby helping him to understand better the nature and the progress of his own experience. It's helpful, for instance, for the skeptical, analytical type to see meditation through the eyes of the poet (William Blake, for instance) or maybe the ecstatic verses of the Psalmist, to see if there is anything in their recorded experiences to match their own, at least, from a purely human standpoint. Or the devoutly religious can obviously find merit in the lyricism of Whitman or Wordsworth as well as in the findings of the scientists. The terminology and concepts of each discipline help to support and illuminate the subject as a whole.

For instance, in Psalm 23 of the Old Testament, what we have here seems to be a brief description of both the method and the benefits of meditation, couched, of course, in religious, poetic language. People, no matter what their religious (or no) beliefs, can read this Psalm with great profit by simply translating it into their own frame of reference. Certainly, everybody can be moved by the dignity and poetry of the language which, essentially, is a joyful affirmation of the value of human life lived in the "green pastures" of contemplation. The psalm is as follows:

1. The Lord is my shepherd; I shall not want.

2. He maketh me to lie down in green pastures; he leadeth me beside the still waters.

3. He restoreth my soul; he leadeth me in the paths of righteousness for his name's sake.

4. Yea, though I walk through the valley of shadow of death, I will fear no evil; for thou art with me; thy rod and thy staff they comfort me.

5. Thou preparest a table before me in the presence of mine enemies; thou annointest my head with oil; my cup runneth over.

6   Surely, goodness and mercy shall follow me all the days of my life; and I will dwell in the house of the Lord for ever. (King James Version)

As for the method, religious or agnostic beliefs become irrelevant in this context because thought is unnecessary in meditation. We need only be like passive lambs, leaping beyond thought to the still waters of the mind by following, not leading. This is why, to religious, meditation (in the sense of contemplation) may seem like a supernatural event because, as St John of the Cross makes clear in his commentaries, it can only take place when the faculties are suspended in their operations and are "passive", meaning that the experience of transcendence cannot take place through the normal and natural use of the mental faculties; rather, St. John says, it can only take place through divine intervention. But to assume that this is a supernatural event and not natural to the human nervous system is just that: an assumption. It presumptuously rules out, in the name of religious authority, that it could also be a natural ability of the mind. Whether this is another case of unexamined, religious dogma or not is very tempting to discuss at this point but may be wisely left for another time and another book. The important thing to stress here is that meditation and its benefits are for real, no matter what one believes.

The Psalmist suggests, then, that meditation offers serenity and contentment to the human spirit, a feeling of completeness and fullness in life. It removes fear and anxiety and encourages better behavior toward our fellow man because of its loving effect on mind and heart. It gives one the feeling of unshakable security and a strong confidence in and affirmation of life. "Though I walk through the valley of the shadow of death, I will fear no evil." Even though expressed in this rhapsodic language, which may tend to trouble the hard-nosed sensibilities of the skeptic, the essential content of the statement is true as the regular practice of meditation will verify: Meditation offers us freedom from fear, freedom from nagging worries that sap the spirit and wear us down even physically. Our confidence grows that life is good and will get better: "Surely goodness and mercy shall follow me all the days of my life." Life seems like a banquet: "Thou preparest a table before me in the presence of mine enemies. My cup runneth over." Life is a feast.

The main point to remember, of course, is that this high peak of blissful feeling, this strong sense of confidence in and affirmation of life (in a permanent sense) is achieved only gradually over a period of time when this attitude, the result of expanded consciousness, finally becomes a routine feature of the waking state, but it's a gradual process. For its sweetest taste and aroma, life, like the best wine, needs time.

Ironically, however, the very slowness of the development is in itself a benefit. As we see life getting better, slowly but surely, we have the privilege of just enjoying each step of the way and not worrying about how long the journey will be. This positive attitude spontaneously grows from the regular practice of meditation, producing this carefree, almost child-like feeling of trust and hope in the goodness and value of life.

This is the common perception of meditators, the feeling of safety, the feeling of warmth and support, a feeling of being at home in an orderly, loving and purposeful world even though they may not be able to explain rationally how they arrived at this conclusion when the world may seem to others sad and dreary (perhaps understandably so in this day and age). Maybe the reason is that the experience in meditation is one of order and security. As the mind settles down and we experience that inner reality of the Self, the totality of our being in untroubled calm, then a growing and all-fulfilling sense of inner peace, confidence and security in life is inevitable. The knowledge, therefore, of the Self, the inner You, is the experience of the full manifestation and joy of living.

Then as the mind grows in this inner sense of serenity and orderliness, behavior automatically begins to improve. In other words, as a person through meditation becomes more in touch with himself, he becomes more in sync with the nobler instincts of his nature. His behavior spontaneously gets better. This is, of course, another basic teaching underlying most systems of meditation down through the ages. It's based on the fundamental belief that man in the deepest part of his nature is good, that all he needs for right action is the full integration of mind and heart which the regular practice of meditation spontaneously fosters.

This same theme of order, security, and a sense of freedom from fear as the result of transcending to the "roots" of one's being is developed in the Chinese classic, the Tao-te-ching, (The Way and its Virtue). The traditional view is that the book was written by Lao Tzu (551-479 B.C.), an older contemporary of Confucius. A very brief treatise, with only five thousand Chinese characters or so, it has had a profound influence on Chinese thought and the whole history of the mystical way despite its extreme brevity. Actually, its conciseness is, in itself, an example of Lao Tzu's philosophy of minimizing action. For Lao Tzu, right action is mostly the result of living in harmony with the natural order which one can know by "holding firmly to stillness", as the following excerpt from Book I of the Tao illustrates:

> I do my utmost to attain emptiness;
> I hold firmly to stillness.
> The myriad creatures all rise together
> And I watch for their return.
> The teeming creatures
> All return to their separate roots.
> RETURNING TO ONE'S ROOTS IS KNOWN AS STILLNESS.
> This is what is meant by returning to one's destiny.
> Returning to one's destiny is known as the constant.
> Knowledge of the constant is known as discernment.
> Woe to him who willfully innovates
> while ignorant of the constant.
> But should one act from knowledge of the constant,
> One's action will lead to impartiality,
> Impartiality to kingliness,
> Kingliness to heaven,
> Heaven to the way,
> The way to perpetuity
> And to the end of one's days
> One will meet with no danger.

Lao Tzu is not advocating passive neglect or a kind of laissez-faire philosophy but rather the thesis that right decisions in life, truly discerning and impartial judgments, must spring from the full depth of man's being; but if man doesn't return to his roots, he is doomed, a notion of which our polluted, aggressive and commercialized society of today could well take heed. The so-called progress of our industrial civilization, as it ravages the environment and creates hostilities among nations, is a good example of a "rootless" society. Right action, whether on a governmental or personal level, does not mean no action at all but of having the wisdom of knowing when to act and when to leave well enough alone. The ability, however, to do this cannot be learned from books but, according to Lao Tzu, by "holding firmly to stillness."

This is purely a philosophical belief with no religious overtones. It's merely a call for man to identify himself with, to merge with the Principle (li) which underlies the world of Nature and Man himself, thereby putting Man in harmony with the fundamental laws of the universe.

The belief in the eternal Self, or the roots of one's being, is almost universal among the Hindus but again with both a theistic as well as an atheistic outlook. The oldest speculation, however, is religious in nature. Written in prose about the tenth century B.C., it is contained in the first great work of Vedic literature, entitled, "Satapatha-Brahmana," from which the following is an excerpt:

> THE BRAHMAN (The underlying power of the cosmos)
>
> Let him meditate upon the true Brahman. Now, man here, indeed, is possessed of understanding, and according to how great his

understanding is when he departs this world, so does he, on passing away, enter yonder world.

Let him meditate on the Self, which is made up of intelligence, and endowed with a body of spirit, with a form of light, and with an ethereal nature, which changes its shape at will, is swift as thought, of true resolve, and true purpose, which consists of all sweet odors and tastes, which holds sway over all the regions, and pervades this whole universe, which is speechless and indifferent; even as a grain of rice, or a grain of barley, or a grain of millet, so is this golden Parusa in the heart; even as a smokeless light, it is greater than the sky, greater than the ether, greater than the earth, greater than all existing things; THAT SELF OF THE SPIRIT IS MYSELF; on passing away from hence, I shall become that Self. Verily, whosoever has this trust, for him there is no uncertainty.[1]

The eloquence of this Vedic passage is particularly moving just as, despite its ancient origin, its theology is brilliant and sophisticated, not much different, basically, from the teaching of Sankara, the great Hindu theologian and metaphysician, whose renowned commentaries on the Veda were written eighteen hundred years later.

The reader, however, may have different reactions. What to some may seem eloquent and poetic, to others may seem like religious bombast. But behind the rhetoric, there is a simple teaching, similar in theme to Psalm 23 or Lao Tzu, namely, that meditation puts us in touch with the very roots of our nature, the Self, where reside all wisdom, intelligence and bliss. Furthermore, this message seems essentially the same throughout the ages in most other religious and philosophical traditions, too numerous to outline here.

CHAPTER 3

SOME PRACTICAL HINTS

POSTURE: The basic problem with the issue of posture in meditation is that there are more unsubstantiated opinions on the subject than there are valid, scientific studies. For instance, there has been no study, to anyone's knowledge, to verify whether or not meditation is more effective when the meditator assumes a certain, prescribed posture, as in Zen meditation, than when he just sits comfortably in an easy chair. This is something the meditator may want to find out for himself by comparing the two postures and seeing whether the one or the other seems to make any difference. But even the world-renowned Zen master, Katsuki Sekida, will tell you in his book on Zen Training:

> It is a fact that one can get into samadhi even sitting in an easy chair in a casual posture, and there are many examples of sick people, confined to bed, who have attained maturity in Zen.[1]

But if you ever made it a point to compare both position in a valid test, you may only find that the Zen position, though impressive, serves no useful purpose. Its only effect is to cause some initial discomfort (and the illusion of progress as you learn to sit without discomfort in the Zen manner). The reason why Zen places so much attention on correct posture and breathing is to prevent the mind from wandering during meditation. As Master Sekida says in his book:

How can we prevent our thoughts from wandering? How can we learn to focus our attention on one thing? The answer is that we cannot do it with our brain alone; the brain cannot control its thoughts by itself. The power to control the activity of our mind comes from the body, and it depends critically on posture and breathing.[2]

If you accept that premise, then it makes sense to sit in a rigid posture because it is true, an attentive posture helps to focus the mind. Mind and body work together. But the purpose of meditation is not to focus the mind, not to prevent it from wandering but to allow it just to be and to flow. When this attitude is assumed, then it attains samahdi (transcends) automatically because it naturally gravitates towards the center of greatest happiness which is the absolute bliss of Itself. It doesn't have to be pushed to do what comes to it naturally. It always seeks the greatest Good.

The purpose, therefore, of meditation is not to reach samahdi by forcing thoughts out because, by trying to force the mind in this way, we tend in fact to inhibit, not promote samahdi. We should neither try to force thoughts out that arise spontaneously nor should we try to deliberately think thoughts. We just don't volunteer any effort one way or the other. If thoughts come on their own, fine, if they don't, fine. All we must do is simply do nothing.

The purpose of meditation is to allow the mind in the waking state to experience transcendental consciousness. It is to bring the two levels of consciousness, the waking state and the transcendental, into close proximity to one another and, finally, into complete, permanent and harmonious union. But in the beginning stages, this is a tentative operation because, as explained, the one tends, to a certain extent, to overshadow the other. For instance, when the mind transcends, when it is absorbed in the Self (or the Holy Spirit, however you may wish to express it), thinking either stops altogether or is reduced to a minimum but this is simply how it is in the early stages of spiritual formation. It is not a goal in itself. The goal of meditation is not to wipe out thinking, the normal activity of the waking state. No, the purpose is to bring the waking state into a working relationship with the transcendental. Meanwhile, it would be imprudent for one to evaluate what is really a sign of imperfect development as an ultimate achievement.

So in the elementary grades, so to speak, of meditation, when the mind transcends, it is hard to think. This is called the ligature, the binding of the faculties. But some meditation guides in the past have deduced from this that if we can help the mind to stop thinking, then it can more easily transcend. This is, of course, an absurd conclusion and it is as widely disseminated by learned masters as it is absurd. The effort to keep the mind from thinking through rigid postures and controlled breathing produces more frustration than transcendence.

It is also an incorrect belief that when the mind ceases to think in meditation that this is the only sign that it is transcending. As discussed, thinking may, indeed, be blocked when the mind is in samahdi but the novice meditator will also have many experiences when the mind will experience both thinking and samahdi simultaneously. This, of course, in due time will become a permanent experience when, through the regular practice of meditation, the nervous system will have gradually expanded its capacity to sustain both levels of function in harmonious union. Before that blissful development, however, there will be only temporary occurrences of this, but it would be foolhardy, indeed, for us to become discouraged over the fact that this illumined state is initially so unpredictable and short-lived. Rather, we should become encouraged because each blissful event is like a beacon of hope, giving us a glorious glimpse of what life will be like in the unitive state of consciousness.

Some people claim that they can meditate lying down. If that is true for them, all well and good, but for most people this position would tend to bring on sleep since, obviously, this is how people customarily take their rest, not that it is impossible to fall asleep sitting down. The point is, simply, that the seated position is more normal for the waking state, just as lying down is for sleeping. But since the body ordinarily reacts according to the position we place it in, we will usually tend to remain awake if we sit up or tend to get drowsy if we lie down.

Those, therefore, who may prefer to lie down during meditation would do well to try it for a while in a seated position. Otherwise, they could be deceiving themselves into thinking they are meditating when, in fact, they may be only experiencing a kind of dull-wakeful or half-dozing state. Full wakefulness is necessary for correct meditation. Though there is some relaxation derived from taking a nap, it is hardly the profound relaxation of meditative bliss. It would be wrong to confuse the one with the other.

So we can't be casual about the position we take. Even though it may not be necessary to sit in a rigidly prescribed manner, it certainly is imperative not to lean back (with feet thrown up on the desk, for instance) but sit up in a normal, seated position.

In religious communities, where kneeling in prayer may be the tradition, this position demands too much expenditure of effort to keep the body erect. There should be no physical effort involved in meditation just as there should be no mental effort because when we try or strain in any way, the mind's natural tendency to transcend is ordinarily inhibited.

BREATHING: As already mentioned, there is no need to control breathing. Within the very first few minutes of the meditation, without any conscious effort, breathing automatically becomes softer and slower until, well into the meditation, a casual observer could think the meditator was not breathing at all. But all this happens spontaneously, not by any controlled effort, as suggested by Zen Master Sekida. It spontaneously occurs as the physical reflection of the mental state. As the mind transcends and experiences inner peace, the body also experiences deep relaxation and lowered metabolic rate because mind and body affect one another. The heart rate, therefore, decreases and blood pressure lowers, if it is high to begin with, just to mention a few of the physiological effects of the meditation. The health benefits, therefore, are obvious because as stress is eliminated through deep relaxation, so also are the many ailments which stress often causes.

FALLING ASLEEP: No matter what happens during meditation, it is always for the good of the body or the mind. If a person drops off to sleep during his meditation, he (or she) should not think that it was a failure, or if it happens regularly, that he cannot meditate at all. It simply means, usually, the obvious: He needs to catch up on his sleep. The answer then to the difficulty is for one to recognize that it is, in fact, not a difficulty. The meditator should simply enjoy the nap but afterwards, when he awakes refreshed, he is ready to continue the meditation, if time is still available. It would be an exercise in futility, however, for one to try to force oneself to stay awake (or, as in Zen meditation groups, allow someone to whack you on the shoulders when he sees you dropping off to sleep). One can't meditate when the body is fatigued and needs sleep. Meditation must take place in the waking state.

If anything, falling asleep is a sign of success, not failure in the meditation. Meditation provides deepest, possible relaxation, thereby unwinding the knots of accumulated stresses within the nervous system and providing whatever healing grace is needed, including sleep. Falling asleep, moreover, during meditation is much more refreshing than an ordinary nap.

Insomniacs can be greatly benefited by meditating on a regular basis with the gradual release of the tensions that may be causing the insomnia.

But if insomnia is not the problem, another possible, reason for chronic sleeping during meditation could be the lack of regular exercise in one's daily regimen. A simple, daily walk is the answer. Some drugs may also have the same effect and the answer to that problem is obvious.

So napping or dozing off during meditation is not a sign of failure but simply an indication that the nervous system is over-burdened with built-up fatigue.

BODILY MOVEMENTS DURING MEDITATION: As already noted, it is not necessary to maintain a rigid stillness throughout the meditation. This is a common misconception. In fact, any attempt to maintain a rigid position would require so much concentration and strain that the outcome would be the exact opposite of what we would expect in meditation: tension and stress instead of a sense of peace and harmony.

It is normal to want to shift position to get comfortable, scratch an itch, yawn or whatever. These movements in no way interfere with the progress and success of the meditation anymore than the bodily shifts and turns we make at night disturb our sleep. A common occurrence is an occasional, deep sigh. Because the breathing is so shallow during the meditation, owing to the body's lowered need for oxygen, the nervous system will automatically trigger a deep sigh, not to increase oxygen intake as with yawning, but to keep the lungs properly distended. This is called the sigh-reflex. It is also a sure, physical sign of deep relaxation during meditation.

There will also be other spontaneous movements as the result of certain, tense muscles relaxing. For instance, sometimes the head will move spontaneously but gently from side to side as the result of tense, neck muscles slowly un-winding, or maybe, for the same reason, there'll be a light muscle spasm (a twitch) in other parts of the body.

Obviously, there is no need for concern over these movements in the mistaken belief that something is wrong and that they must be somehow suppressed. Far from being any kind of problem to be dealt with, they are a symptom of something good happening as the nervous system releases stress. We should regard them with the same laissez-faire attitude as we should with the spontaneous movements of the mind such as day-dreams, distractions and mind-wanderings.

HEADACHES DURING MEDITATION: The usual reason for a headache developing during meditation is that the meditator is straining in some way. Usually, this symptom is associated with the methods of meditation that use the repetition of a phrase or sound, or concentration on a single thought and the like. The meditator has been led to believe that if he focuses hard enough on what he is thinking, he will attain samahdi. But what he gets, instead, is a head-ache. This focused concentration is exactly what the recipe for meditation does NOT prescribe. Meditation, correctly done, will quickly cure a headache, not cause one.

TIMING THE MEDITATION: Obviously, you can't be looking at the clock every two minutes to see what time it is. All you have to do is roughly estimate it and when you think you have finished, just open your eyes and glance at your watch. This will in no way disturb the meditation. If you see that your time is up, then all you need do is close the eyes again and come out slowly. If you see there is more time left, then, of course, simply continue. Again, the brief interruption has no disturbing effect. It makes no difference if you go over the allotted time a few minutes. But don't use a timer: It will only serve as an unnecessary distraction. You will always be thinking of when it might go off. A rough estimation, therefore, is all that's necessary.

ENDING THE MEDITATION: You should not end the meditation abruptly. You can't just pop up suddenly from the depth of meditation and then just go about your business. The transition from this most profound level of relaxation into normal activity should be gradual. You should take two or three minutes to come out. That means, when you decide to end the meditation, you don't just stop and abruptly get up. You should remain seated with eyes closed, maybe stretch a little, start the mind going first by actively thinking of something (like what you're going to do next), rub the eyes perhaps, take a few deep breaths and so forth. Then after you've sat a few minutes doing just that, you simply get up and return to normal activity. This is important because, otherwise, an abrupt transition can make you feel irritable and uncomfortable for a while after the meditation though this condition gradually dissipates.

NEGATIVE FEELINGS: Any negative feelings that may arise during the meditation may seem inconsistent with the picture we all have of it as being a peaceful and harmonious experience. But again - and this principle cannot be overemphasized - it is the very depth of the relaxation that, ironically, is the occasional cause of some discomfort as pent-up tensions unwind and are released. The meditation then can become the escape-valve for old or new feelings of repressed hostility, anxiety or anger. The meditator is then forced to face them once again but in the relaxed and safe atmosphere of the meditation. He (or she) relives them but not for the sake of reviving old wounds but for the sake of facing them, healing them and forgetting them. All this, of course, happens spontaneously. One never knows from one meditation to the next when this kind of stress-release will occur but when it does, it is always for the good.

SEXUAL FEELINGS ARISING DURING MED-ITATION: Again, it may seem surprising to some, especially religious people, that sexual arousal could come during meditation. This happens sometimes simply because the body is as much a part of the meditation as the mind. When the mind is deeply relaxed, for instance, the body is as well. They are not separate entities but act as one. So when the mind transcends and experiences exaltation, the body could also parallel that feeling in its own way through sexual arousal. Not that this happens on a regular basis, but it seems to be a rational explanation of this experience. Religious, of course, would have a great deal of difficulty with this because they would feel it necessary to drive out the "impure thoughts." But all the effort to do so would only increase the problem (so-called) by making them more conscious of it as they struggle to drive "the impure thoughts" away.

But these sexual thoughts come spontaneously and will depart spontaneously, but even if they don't, actively trying to drive them out just doesn't work. And religious who may feel guilty about the fact God made man a sexual creature, should not be. If the feeling of sexual arousal came quite innocently of its own initiative, as it were, and not by any conscious choice, there can be no moral culpability. Those who accept their sexuality as normal and healthy will, of course, see no moral problem.

MEDITATION AND DIGESTION: It's not a good idea to study right after a heavy meal. The same reasoning applies also to meditation. Of course, if you are hungry just before meditation and you must meditate right away, then a light snack to quiet the hunger pangs should not make any difference. Some people like to have their coffee as soon as they wake up in the morning, but if you are a meditator, it would be preferable to hold off on the coffee since it is a stimulant which would be in conflict with the meditation. Not that it's impossible to meditate after a cup or two. It's just that it's better to try to get maximum results from each meditation and not impede it in anyway. Some would say that coffee would not make any appreciable difference. Maybe not, but who can really say? A safer more conservative choice would be to have the discipline to put off having your coffee until after the meditation.

ALCOHOL, DRUGS AND MEDITATION: The same advice would also apply to other stimulants, and also to depressants such as alcohol. Many people like to enjoy a drink or two to relax after a hard day's work. For a meditator, however, the most relaxing thing to do would be first to meditate before having a drink although abstinence is always the better course for those who may have difficulty holding the high ground of moderation. Alcohol doesn't make meditation impossible, though it tends to get in the way since the physical system must waste energy in detoxifying the bloodstream rather than for more useful purposes.

Too much drink, in fact, dulls the mind, the senses and the feelings or can make some people hostile and aggressive. It is in no way comparable to the more delightful "intoxication" of the meditation. If we want to feel some conviviality after a long day's work, we don't need alcohol. No amount of it helps the meditation, nor does it, unless it's taken in moderation, help the meditator.

The same principle applies to other drugs such as marijuana, cocaine and the like. They are not helpful aids in the meditation, as some may erroneously believe, any more than their depressing after-effects. As for those who think that LSD or other hallucinogens may also be somehow help-ful in meditation, how can they possibly make any rational connection between hallucinations and the mind tran-scending? The purpose of meditation is not to be entertained with fascinating images or visions, but to transcend from images to the Silence within.

Though drugs may not help the meditation, meditation can help the drug addict or the alcoholic, not only as a powerful, natural instrument of detoxification but as a staunch support and comforting aid in the withdrawal process. This, of course, destroys the myth that a person can't meditate unless he or she is completely off drugs to begin with, advice which is not too comforting to the addict. It's a myth somewhat reminiscent of the counsel of some religious advisors who assert that the gift of contemplation is not given to the imperfect.

HOW LONG SHOULD ONE MEDITATE? Some meditation schools, such as the International Meditation Society, recommend for beginners in meditation fifteen to twenty minutes each session, twice a day, once in the morning before breakfast and again in late afternoon or early evening before the evening meal. The Society suggests that the amount of time could be increased gradually so that maybe, after two or three years of meditation, one could meditate for forty-five minutes each time. All this seems, of course, quite specific though there are other meditation groups that don't seem concerned with the time factor. Religious orders, however, traditionally set aside in their community schedule a certain, specified amount of time for meditation, usually a half-hour to an hour.

Meditation is good medicine but too much medicine is not necessarily good. A life of meditation with little or no activity is not, obviously, right or advisable. The purpose of meditation is not to retreat from life but to give it a solid foundation, a positive depth and direction. The key word, then, in the discussion is balance, a balance between activity and the daily practice of meditation, resulting in the full development of consciousness through the gradual merger of the waking state with the deep restfulness of the contemplative. That is why activity is a necessary and integral part of the process.

Unless one, therefore, is on retreat or on vacation, it is probably best not to indulge in excessively long meditations. As we know, meditation slows down the metabolism and the mental faculties. After a short meditation, however, this binding effect on the faculties quickly disappears, but after a prolonged one, it may be noticed that it's somewhat difficult to concentrate or to keep up one's normal pace of activity. Even though this effect too will pass, it will not pass as quickly as perhaps one would want. It could be a problem for some while after the meditation, if one's occupation requires a lot of concentration. There could also be some feelings of irritability (which is not exactly a desirable effect of meditation). It is better, therefore, to keep our meditation time within comfortable limits.

In a retreat, however, where meditation time can be increased as much as desired, it's still a good idea to moderate it with intervals of activity. Rather than meditating uninterruptedly most of the day, a series of meditations would be the better idea, each one followed by ten minutes or so of mild exercises such as slow walking, stretching (yoga or otherwise) and the like. Each meditation in the series should be no longer than the amount of time one ordinarily spends for it. Again, this routine is simply a sensible application of the principle of the need for balancing meditation with activity. Strenuous activity, however, like jogging, push-ups, swimming and the like would not be recommended during retreat. This kind of movement would be too much of a stress on the physical system because of the dramatic lowering of the metabolic rate from increased meditations.

You could meditate all day in the manner described above and even into the early evening, if so desired, depending, on how much time you have. But here the principle of not too much too soon applies. On the first day of the retreat, it would be wiser to begin slowly by adding just one extra meditation to your normal quota of two a day, then, on each successive day, adding one more. Midway in the retreat, however, you should reverse the procedure by eliminating one meditation each day until on the final day you have returned to your normal routine of two a day (assuming two a day to be your normal routine).

Even having done this, you should be particularly careful while driving home from the retreat house. This is not to imply there is any great danger involved. It is simply a matter of taking a little extra precaution under the circumstances, as you emerge from a long period of silence and deep relaxation into the hurly-burly of speeding traffic.

WHERE TO MEDITATE: It is possible to meditate in almost any environment even on a sidewalk bench, for instance, amidst downtown traffic. No one is recommending this as preferable, but simply to point out that normal noise, at least, what we consider in this day and age to be normal, doesn't interfere with the meditation. Though it's traditional to seek a relatively quiet spot to meditate such as your room or private office, this kind of solitude is not necessary. Moreover, the routine noises you may hear from the outside in the privacy of your room or office are not, in fact, a hindrance to the meditation. That's why those isolation tanks some people use for meditating, though impressive and expensive, are unnecessary. Some people, however, believe that some religious or mood music in the background may be helpful. But, ironically, unlike background noise, its attractive charm can be a problem. It can cause an internal struggle between the mind's natural tendency to dive within (transcend) and the music's tendency to keep it on the surface. Among all the possible distractions imaginable, as your own experience may prove, only music can have this effect, (except for trying to meditate with eyes open). Music can be deeply moving, but we must not confuse a pleasant, sensual experience with the deeper experience of transcending. The following is an excerpt from St. John of the Cross on the subject:

> If a person strives for recreation of his appetites and for sensory satisfaction, he will rather encounter spiritual dryness and distraction, because spiritual satisfaction and contentment is found only in interior recollection.[3]

Again:

> When a person, therefore, prays in a beautiful
> site, he should endeavor to be interiorly with
> God and forget the place, as though he were
> not there at all. For when people wander about
> looking for delight and gratification from a
> particular site, they are in search, as we said,
> for sensory recreation and spiritual instability
> more than spiritual tranquillity.[4]

THE PHYSICAL AND MENTAL SIGNS OF ME-
DITATION: There are certain physical and mental
indications by which one can determine whether he or she is
meditating correctly or not. On the physical level, for
instance, the clearest indicator is that the breath rate slows
down usually to the point where a casual observer may not
be able to tell whether the meditator is breathing or not. But
this need not be the case in every meditation. As long as there
is some decrease in breath rate, this is sign enough. (Then, as
mentioned, there is the sigh-reflex which may occur from
time to time). As already explained, some meditations may
seem more profound than others depending on the stress-
release factor. There would also be some corresponding
decrease in heart-beat and blood-pressure.

Another good sign is a feeling of deep relaxation
throughout the whole body and, as discussed in another
context, that deep relaxation could cause some muscular
twitching. The head may also spontaneously start to move
gently from side to side or end up drooped down to the chest,
but these are simply physical signs of profound repose and
release of stress.

Some meditators, especially in the beginning phase of
the practice, often experience a warm, tingling feeling in the
extremities (as if a hand or foot had gone to sleep). This is

due to the relaxed dilation of the blood vessels and increased volume of blood-flow. That feeling of warmth could also radiate throughout the whole body. (If you have a sweater on, for instance, you may find yourself getting warm and may want to take it off).

Then there are other signs which we could call mental or spiritual signs. For instance, one usually becomes aware of an inner feeling of peace and contentment that may remain throughout the entire meditation with varying degrees of intensity or may be felt only intermittently. (During the so-called restless meditation, it can also be experienced but, of course, somewhat dulled by the release of stress). As already mentioned, this peaceful state also tends to inhibit mental function. Yet, as also previously discussed, that peacefulness could be interrupted from time to time with various distractions or day-dreams. In actual fact, the meditator is always deeply relaxed whether he or she is fully aware of it or not because, as stress is released, the subjective feeling of relaxation may vary in its intensity, depending upon the intensity of the release. Understandably, beginning medita-tors may have some difficulty with this.

The ligature of the mental faculties may bring about other effects as well. A person, for instance, could lose all track of time. A twenty minute meditation could seem like five or the reverse could be true; sometimes five minutes could seem like twenty. Also, thinking beyond the simplest of notions could be difficult such as trying to remember some-thing one knows very well he or she could easily remember outside the meditation. Moreover, whatever thinking may go on would be usually trivial or dream-like in quality. Paradox-ically, however, amidst this incoherency of ideas and images, there could be a sudden flash of an idea, an insight or the unexpected solution to a long-standing problem. But a word of caution: One should never assume that just because the idea came during meditation that it should be infallibly trusted. It should always be reviewed, after the meditation, in the bright light of the normal, waking state.

The same reasoning also applies to so-called "visions" that may come. If there is such a thing as a genuine vision, we must, at least, make sure that it is not the product of some heavy stress-release, a delayed drug-reaction or an over-worked imagination.

Sometimes one may experience a complete absence of all thought and self-awareness though fully awake. This is a most profound experience of transcendence, in which the nervous system is deeply at rest while still remaining in the waking state, though the individual may later think he or she was asleep or wonder where he or she has been, having lost all track of time and consciousness of one's surroundings. This temporary state of mind, however, is very pleasant and should not be frightening. It's simply an experience of very deep, transcendent rest.

How you feel after a meditation is another indicator that you are meditating correctly. For instance, you may sense an increase of energy and a relaxed, get-up-and-go interest in life, like a renewal, or if you felt anxious or irritable before the meditation, you will no longer feel that way afterwards, or much less so. Everything will seem brighter, more interesting, more carefree and effortless and as you continue to meditate, life, in general, becomes less of an uphill struggle as you become gradually more at peace with yourself and more capable of coping with stress.

MEDITATION AND INSOMNIA: As already discussed, meditations's prime purpose is to expand consciousness to its fullest development. Its major goal, therefore, should not be lost sight of. Yet, it can serve secondary goals as well. Because of its profoundly healing effects, for instance, it can be used as a powerful, natural aid in the recovery process and because of its deeply relaxing effect on the body, it can be extremely helpful both in the case of chronic or occasional insomnia. The proof of this can come from personal experience. When we are feeling restless and tense and we can't seem to fall asleep (or get back to sleep), meditation can easily solve the problem, dramatically proving how deeply relaxing it is to the nervous system. All one has to do, then, is to sit up in bed and meditate for ten minutes or so, thereby releasing the stress and tensions responsible for the sleep disturbance, and then lie down again and notice what happens: Without any trying on our part, sleep will come automatically. If this doesn't work, then another brief meditation will usually do the trick, though most of the time, one should be sufficient.

Ordinarily, however, a regular meditator should be a deep sleeper, because of the overall, stabilizing effect meditation has on the nervous system, but for those times when we occasionally need a little help to get to sleep, pills are unnecessary.

It does not follow, however, that meditating on a regular basis shortly before retiring is a good idea. No, if we are not overstressed, the effect will be the exact opposite. The meditation will energize the system and keep us awake. The technique works only when we find we cannot sleep.

MORNING MEDITATION: Your morning meditation may often seem not as deep as your late afternoon or early evening one, but that subjective feeling can be misleading. Both meditations are equally effective. The reason your morning one may seem shallower than your second one later in the day is based on the fact that the second one comes after a day's activity with its resulting fatigue and stress when the feeling of deep relaxation may seem more obvious...like a warm and welcome bath, as opposed to the morning meditation when we come to it well-rested after a night's sleep and do not notice the contrast as much. The truth is, however, that the effectiveness of each meditation is the same despite what our subjective evaluation may lead us to believe.

MEDITATION AND ILLNESS: The curative value of meditation lies in the fact that, physiologically, it is really a very deep rest, apparently deeper than deep sleep as a 1972 investigation by Doctors Wallace and Benson[5] seemed to show and as confirmed by a similar study by Dr. Corey in 1973.[6] They measured "rest" in terms of oxygen intake. In the resting state we consume less oxygen than when we are active. In deep sleep we consume even less but in the subjects being tested during meditation, the doctors found that the depth of rest they achieved was even deeper than deep sleep because the amount of oxygen consumed during meditation was significantly less than the amount consumed in deep sleep. (But we are awake when we meditate). So when your doctor tells you, as most doctors often do, to get plenty of rest when you are ill, there is no better rest than meditation (although it is not a substitute for needed sleep). So meditating as much as you feel is comfortable for you when you are ill or under the duress of pregnancy seems like a good idea.

But the best cure is not to get sick in the first place. Meditation on a regular basis not only provides very deep rest to the system each time we meditate but tends to create a more restful mode of mental and physical function in general. This less stressed more restful state begets the happy by-product of an over-all strengthening of the immune system or of the body's ability to resist infection. If rest can help cure illness, it can also help prevent it.

PERSEVERANCE; The cultivation of consciousness to reach the full maturity of "restful alertness" is a gradual process. How long it takes, one cannot possibly know but its achievement through the twice daily practice of meditation is inevitable as long as you keep up the practice. A busy person may convince himself that he hasn't time to include meditation into his daily schedule but if he can't, at least, find five minutes in the morning and five later in the late afternoon or early evening, this sad casualty of the work ethic is fast on his way toward some stress-related illness. Certainly, he can do five on a regular basis, and when he slips into that routine, he may soon understand the importance of what he is doing and, quite possibly, the need to increase his meditation time to the recommended twenty or thirty minutes each session.

But time is not lost when we meditate. Since it has the effect of releasing stress, clearing the head and increasing one's energy level, we make up for the time we take out in meditation by functioning more efficiently and getting things done more quickly. But your most important task is to get into the meditation habit, even if, in the beginning, you only meditate five minutes each time. You may want to go easy, at first. Once the habit is established, however, meditation will become as routine as brushing your teeth.

CHAPTER 4

MEDITATION AND THE NEW TESTAMENT

There seems to be abundant evidence that Christ's essential message, through both his word and example, stressed not only the importance of daily prayer for man's spiritual growth, but a kind of prayer that was more contemplative, simple and quiet in nature. For instance, read his analogies on the kingdom of heaven:

> What is the kingdom of God like, and to what shall I liken it? It is like a grain of mustard seed, which a man took and cast into his own garden; and it grew and became a large tree. and the birds of the air dwelt in its branches. (St. Luke, 13:18-19).

Also:

> To what shall I liken the kingdom of God? It is like leaven, which a woman took and buried in three measures of flour, until all of it was leavened. (St. Luke, 13: 20-21).

These statements seem to emphasize that the kingdom of God, which Christ said is within us, (Luke, 17: 21), lies hidden within the human spirit like a seed or leaven and grows, under the proper condition, quite naturally like the mustard tree and the leavened bread. Obviously, the condition is that the seed must be left alone in the soil just as the leaven in the flour must be left undisturbed. From this passive, quiet state, the mustard tree grows and the bread rises, passivity being the basis of their transformation. If the analogy is applied to man's spiritual growth, the quietness and passivity of contemplative prayer seems to be what he is referring to. As the seed and the leavened bread need quietness to grow or rise, so also does man need the silence of contemplative prayer, on a regular basis, for his spiritual transformation toward the bliss of divine union, ...or to reach the kingdom of God that lies within him.

If the above interpretation seems somewhat far-fetched, it may seem less so when you consider Christ's emphatic teaching that prayer should be brief and simple in content, that it should be a private thing, conducted, for example, in the secrecy and quietness of one's room. He rejected the verbosity and ostentation of public prayer. Recall when he said:

> Moreover, when you are at prayer, do not use many phrases, like the heathens, who think to make themselves heard by their eloquence. You are not to be like them; your heavenly Father knows well what your needs are before you ask him. (Matthew, 6:7-9)

This also echoes Isaias in the Old Testament "....and when you multiply prayer, I will not hear." (Isaias,1:15). And since God knows what we need even before we ask him, Christ seems to be saying that the prayer of petition is simply unnecessary. In one stroke, then, he wiped out the need for most vocal prayers recited or sung in public places of worship.

> When thou prayest, go into thy room, and closing the door, pray to thy Father in secret: and thy Father, who sees in secret, will reward thee. (Matthew,6:6).

Then he gave an explicit example, in the "Our Father", of how prayer should be: brief and simple in content, and since, as noted, he was against public, vocal and especially long-winded prayer, it may be reasonable to presume that he did not intend the "Our Father", as it often is, to be vocalized verbatim, or even worse, by rote. It seems more likely it was meant to serve simply as an illustration of a basic principle that prayer should be simple in content, not a model to be slavishly repeated.

It may be in keeping with his theory, then, if during prayer we just sat thinking a simple phrase from the "Our Father" such as "Thy kingdom come" in an effortless, passive-receptive manner. Indeed, the mental verbalization of the phrase may not even be necessary, as personal experience will prove, nor, for that matter, any other phrase of the "Our Father." What seems necessary is simply putting into practice what the prayer suggests, namely, a passive posture of child-like trust as we await in prayer the coming and the comfort of the Holy Spirit from within. "Thy kingdom come, thy will be done" is the essential message of the prayer. Christ said also, "....unless you turn and become like little children, you will not enter into the kingdom of heaven." But this is a teaching you need not blindly accept just on faith. It can be a matter of your own experience when you adopt this contemplative attitude of child-like trust in prayer.

In addition to his emphasis on the need for simplicity and child-like surrender, Christ also stressed, both by word and example, the importance of praying on a daily basis. The phrase from the Lord's prayer itself, "Give us this day our daily bread", is the first example that springs to mind. Since it's contained within the prayer, it is not unreasonable to assume that Christ was speaking here of the spiritual nourishment of prayer, not actual bread or food. The suggestion seems to be, then, that prayer is to the spirit as bread is to the body: nourishment, strength and sustenance.

And like food, we need prayer on a daily basis. Christ not only made numerous pronouncements on the subject but served as a superb model of what he preached, which the following excerpts from the New Testament amply illustrate:

> Watch, then, praying at all times....(Luke, 21:36).

> And he also told them a parable-that they must always pray and not lose heart... (St. Luke, 18:1)

> Pray without ceasing. Watch, therefore, for you do not know at what hour your Lord is to come. (Matthew 24:42)

> Watch, then, praying at all times... (Luke, 21:36).

> Now it came to pass in those days that he went out to the mountain to pray, and continued all night in prayer to God." (Luke, 6:12-13)

> But he himself was in retirement in the desert, and in prayer." (Luke,5:16)

> Come apart in a desert place and rest awhile. (Mark, 6:31)

> And when he dismissed them, he went away to the mountain to pray.(Mark, 6:46).

> Also: (Luke, 5:42) and (Mark, 14:37).

Furthermore, Christ's message seems to be that this interior growth of the spirit, nourished by prayer, is, like the seed or the leavened bread, automatic and gradual.

> Thus is the kingdom of God: as though a man
> should cast seed into the earth, then sleep and
> rise, night and day, and the seed should
> prosper and grow without his knowing it. For
> of itself the earth bears crop, first the blade,
> then the ear, then the full grain in the ear.
> (Mark, 4: 26-29)

The seed, the symbol of spiritual transformation, is also hidden from view, suggesting those other parables which Christ developed, namely, the parables of the hidden treasure and the pearl of great price which teach that the most important reality of life is the inner dimension of the human spirit.

> The kingdom of heaven is like a treasure
> hidden in a field: he who finds it hides it, and
> in his joy goes and sells all that he has and
> buys that field. Again, the kingdom of heaven
> is like a merchant in search of fine pearls.
> When he finds a single pearl of great price, he
> goes out and sells all that he has and buys it.
> (Matthew, 13:45-46).

The pearl analogy may suggest as well the same idea developed in the mustard-seed and leavened-bread analogies. For instance, the oyster, the most passive of all creatures is, nevertheless, capable of producing from its most humble abode, the pearl of great price. In the silent depth of the sea, it does nothing, yet is transformed into something of immense value. So also, as the parable may seem to suggest, with respect to man's spiritual transformation: The hidden treasure of God's kingdom is discovered and the pearl of enlightenment gradually formed in the silent depth and self-immolation of contemplative prayer.

But even more dramatic is Christ's analogy of the grain of wheat:

> Amen, I say to you, unless the grain of wheat
> falls into the ground and dies, it remains alone.
> But if it dies, it brings forth much fruit. He
> who loves his life, loses it; he who hates his
> life in this world, keeps it unto life
> everlasting." (St. John, 12:24-26).

Traditionally, this notion of dying to one's self is often given an ascetical interpretation by various spiritual writers, the denial consisting in the killing of "the old man" of one's unruly instincts and passions. This is, of course, a desirable goal but too often this has been interpreted to mean that the path to God is primarily through ascetical practices and the immolation of one's unruly passions and inordinate desires by external means such as fasting and penances. But with Christ's repeated emphasis on the need for prayer in daily life, it seems more likely he was talking about an inner, spiritual change of mind and heart, which results from a life of prayer.

The immolation of the self takes place in contemplation. When we just sit quietly, holding in suspense (without trying) all normal, mental function, then, in a true sense, the normal expression of the self is denied as the mind transcends, or, expressing it in religious terms, the self surrenders to the sanctifying influence of the Holy Spirit. Nourished by prayer, man then grows in God-consciousness, enlightened perception, detachment and more compassionate, loving behavior. Spiritual detachment comes as the result of contemplative practice. Striving to bring this about through ascetical means, (whether harsh or mild, it makes no difference), is not possible. You can't force your way into this higher level of consciousness by external devices. It is nourished from within by contemplation, growing gradually and naturally like a plant.

This theory, however, does not rule out the accompanying need for all men to be responsible for their own actions at all times, to look inward, examine conscience, and by direct effort use whatever ascetical practices may be required to overcome bad habits and improve behavior. It merely puts the main emphasis on prayer as the primary, essential catalyst of change. This seems to be a fair interpretation of Christ's message, that it is through prayer, presumably contemplative prayer, that the "dying to one's self" primarily takes place.

Christ continued to drum on this same theme throughout his ministry, sometimes in sombre, puzzling even shocking terms. "Amen, amen I say to thee, unless a man be born again, he cannot see the kingdom of God," he said to Nicodemus (St. John,3:3). Obviously taken back, Nicodemus replied, "How can a man be born when he is old? Can he enter a second time into his mother's womb and be born again? " Then to clarify, Christ said, "Amen, amen I say to thee, unless a man be born again of water and the Spirit, he cannot enter into the kingdom of God. That which is born of the flesh is flesh: and that which is born of the Spirit is spirit. (St.John,3:6)

Mincing no words, therefore, Christ describes in the above quotation the radically different nature of this inner transformation. It's as if one were born again, raised to an enlightened state of consciousness that's totally distinct from the ordinary waking state. So, apparently, the difference is not just a matter of a few shades of grey but as night is from day, as life in the womb is from life after birth, and as the tiniest of seeds, the mustard seed, is from the fully grown tree.

The denial of the self, therefore, is not really a denial or a loss. It is rather a transformation to a higher level of consciousness. It begins when prayer is kept contemplative and not vocal, when conscious activity and self-expression during it is kept to a minimum, or none at all. In this sense is the self denied when we just keep quiet and listen. In religious meditation, therefore, or in contemplation, all one has to do is merely do nothing, just be trusting and still like a child sitting contentedly in its mother's lap.

CHAPTER 5

MEDITATION AND THE OLD TESTAMENT

In the old Testament there are countless references to the need for silence as the absolute essential, the indispensable foundation of religious life through which Man is enabled to commune with his Creator. The most explicit reference of them all would be the phrase taken from Psalm 45:11: "Be still and know that I am God." The Latin uses the word "vacate" which conveys the meaning of "be empty." Regarding this, St. John (of the Cross) has some important comments, which are as follows:

> When the spiritual person cannot meditate, he should learn to remain in God's presence with a loving attention and a tranquil intellect even though he seems to himself to be idle. For little by little and very soon the divine calm and peace with a wondrous, sublime knowledge of God, enveloped in divine love, will be infused into his soul. HE SHOULD NOT INTERFERE WITH FORMS OF DISCURSIVE MEDITATIONS AND IMAGININGS. Otherwise, his soul will be disquieted and drawn out of its peaceful contentment to distaste and repugnance. And if, as we said, scruples about his inactivity arise, he should remember that pacification of soul (making it calm and peaceful, inactive and desireless) is no small accomplishment. This, indeed, is what our Lord asks of us through David: Vacate et videte quoniam ego

sum Deus. (Ps. 45:11) This would be like
saying: Learn to be empty of all things-
interiorly and exteriorly- and you will behold
that I am God.[1]

Other verses from the psalms, similar in theme, are
listed below:

> The Lord will hear me when I call upon Him.
> Tremble and sin not. Reflect upon your beds in
> silence. Ps. 4:5-6, (Confraternity of Christian
> Doctrine translation).

> The Lord is my shepherd; I shall not want. He
> maketh me to lie down in green pastures: He
> restoreth my soul: He leadeth me in the paths
> of righteousness for his name's sake. (Ps.23:1-
> 3, St. James' version).

In this famous psalm, the essence of meditation or
contemplation is defined. Our passive role like sheep is emphasized as the Shepherd leads the way and we simply
follow in silence and submission.

Then in Psalm 130, we read more of the same:

> Oh Lord, my heart is not proud nor are my
> eyes haughty; I busy not myself with great
> things too sublime for me. Nay, rather, I have
> stilled and quieted my soul like a weaned
> child. Like a weaned child on its mother's lap,
> so is my soul within me. (Ps. 130:1-3)

> Had I but wings like a dove, I would fly away
> and be at rest. Far away I would flee; and I
> would lodge in the wilderness. I would hasten
> to find shelter from the violent storm and the
> tempest. (Ps. 54:7-9)

And still more in Isaias:

> Go, my people, enter into thy chambers, shut the doors upon thee, hide thyself for a moment. (Is.26:20)

> For thus saith the Lord, the Holy One of Israel: If you return and be quiet, you shall be saved. In silence and in hope shall your strength be. (Is. 30:15)

> Their strength is to sit still. (Is. 30:7)

Added to the theme of silence, we read in other Old Testament passages the idea of "waiting or watching" in silence such as in Lamentations, 3:24-26):

> Heth: The Lord is my potion, said my soul: therefore will I wait for Him.

> Teth: The Lord is good to them that hope in Him, to the soul that seeketh Him.

> Teth: It is good to wait in silence for the salvation of the Lord.

The same concept is paralleled in yet another Psalm:

> I trust in the Lord; my soul trusts in His word. My soul waits for the Lord more than sentinels wait for the dawn. More than sentinels wait for dawn, let Israel wait for the Lord. (Ps.129:6-7)

> Wait for the Lord; be stouthearted and wait for the Lord. (Ps. 26:14)

In a true sense, contemplation is, indeed, like waiting or watching, not interfering, but passively sitting and waiting in silence for the "coming of the Lord" (or for the mind to transcend).

> Happy the man who obeys me and happy those
> who keep my ways, happy the man watching
> daily at my gates, watching at my door posts
> for he who finds Me finds life. (Prov. 8:32-36)

Watching is similar to waiting but with the emphasis on being alert and wakeful. In contemplation, the mind in the waking state simply watches or "gazes", not at anything in particular, but simply like a sentinel remains passively attenive and watchful. The Holy Spirit, in other words, is not experienced when we are asleep or half-awake. All the above passages then stress that man's bond with God is formed and strengthened in contemplative silence which is described as the patient watchfulness of a sentinel waiting for the dawn.

Not only does the Old Testament recommend the need for waiting for God in silence but He is described as BEING the Silence. He must, therefore, be heard in silence because He is the Silence, like the "whistling of gentle air" or a "still voice", as we read in 3 Kings, (19:11-13, Confraternity Edition):

> And he said to him (Elias): Go forth, and
> stand upon the mount before the Lord. And
> behold the Lord passeth. And a great and
> strong wind before the Lord overthrowing the
> mountains, and breaking the rocks in pieces:
> the Lord is not in the earthquake. And after
> the earthquake a fire: the Lord is not in the
> fire. And after the fire a whistling of a gentle
> air.

Then in Job we read of God as a still voice, "light as a rustling breeze", (Monsignor Knox edition, Sheed and Ward, New York, 1950).

> Listen; here is a secret that was made known
> to me; it was but the breath of a whisper
> overheard. It was the hour when night visions
> breed disquiet, as men lie chained by sleep;
> fear took hold of me, a fit of trembling that
> thrilled my whole frame, and made every hair
> bristle. All at once a spirit came beside me; no
> face I knew, yet I could see the form of it, and
> catch its voice, light as a rustling breeze. (Job,
> 4:12-17)

The teaching, therefore, should be clear: If God is silence, He is experienced in silence, not in the activity of religious externals such as rituals, hymns, or vocal prayers (lengthy or brief) and the like. Religious rites, sermons or hymns may have an uplifting effect emotionally or aesthetically, but their emotional or aesthetic effect should not be confused with the higher experience of the transcendent Reality of the Godhead Who is Silence and is experienced in silence. Hymns and vocal prayers should be the joyful expression of this experience, not the mistaken substitute for it.

We must not confuse the sweet emotions and thoughts about God, heard in church or temple, with the sweeter "emotion" of actually experiencing Him in the silent depth of our minds and hearts. We praise God best when, like children listening to a good story, we just sit quietly in mute acceptance, and allow the deep peace of the Holy Spirit to lighten the burden of our humanity. The best sermon we can hear is the sound of God's still voice, light as a rustling breeze. This is said not to discount the relative values of religious ceremony but simply to suggest we should understand the important difference between what is authentic, religious experience and what is merely its surface expression.

If a person is to enjoy the bliss of divine union, he must allow the mind to transcend the realm of religious rites, prayers, and pious emotions and find God who is defined as lying outside the sphere of all activity. He is Absolute Silence. He is pure Existence and, therefore, in His unmanifest nature, non-active. He is neither activity nor can be known through activity, however pious and well-intentioned it may be. Trying to visualize Him, for instance, in some way or hold prayerful conversations with Him may be of some psychological comfort but the greatest comfort would come when the talking stops, the attempt to visualize Him ceases, and the mind in contemplative silence, tastes the sweetness of His quiet Presence deep within the very core of its being. Again, on this point, St. John is most helpful:

> To reach this essential union of love with God, a person must be careful not to lean upon imagination, visions, forms, figures or particular ideas, since they cannot serve as a proportionate and proximate means for such an effect - they would instead be a hindrance.[2]

The word "religion" is from the Latin whose root meaning is to "bind" or "form a bond" and it's essentially in contemplation where the word is truly defined, where the loving bond between Man and his Creator is formed in the very depth of the human spirit.

CHAPTER 6

SOME RELIGIOUS IMPLICATIONS

There is an unmistakable connection between this form of meditation and the Catholic Church's teaching on "infused contemplation" because absolute passivity is recommended in both cases. By "infused contemplation" is meant simply that the individual, sitting quietly in prayer, does nothing but remain passive and receptive, thus allowing the Holy Spirit to "pour in" or "infuse" His graces into the soul. For beginners, however, this total passivity, is not recommended by the Church but only for those advanced in the "spiritual life" and only after it has been determined by a competent spiritual counselor that they have been divinely called to this higher level of prayer. Those, however, who would attempt contemplation without proper counsel would, supposedly, be leaving themselves open to self-deception and spiritual sloth. As St. Theresa of Avila, the great Spanish mystic and reformer of the Church, said:

> God gave us faculties that we might use them;
> each of them will receive its proper reward.
> Do not let us then try to charm them to sleep:
> let us permit them to do their work until
> divinely called to something higher.[1]

In addition, there is a possibility that the Church would regard this passive approach as "Quietism", a teaching of Madam Guyon's, in sixteenth century France. It's a teaching which the Church at that time vehemently condemned, recommending instead more activity during prayer such as affective acts, pious reflections, prayerful aspirations of gratitude, worship, love, acts of contrition and the like.

This would be called discursive meditation as described by St. John of the Cross when he wrote:

> The beginner uses discursive exercises and acts with the imagination. In this state, it is necessary for the soul to be given material for meditation and reasoning, and it is well for it to make interior acts on its own account.[2]

An easier method of meditation, however, is also authorized by the Church, and that is the one taught by St. Theresa of Avila who was a contemporary and highly esteemed friend of St. John's. Though along with him she did not recommend absolute passivity for beginners, neither did she advocate cluttering the mind with too many ideas or making too much of an effort. Similar to St.Ignatius' method, to be considered shortly, she suggested to her sisters that they meditate on the "Our Father" and take even a whole hour of the meditation period to consider it. So for beginners, her emphasis is on simplicity of thought, seemingly no analysis, and a more effortless, non-discursive approach toward prayer. She wrote:

> If once we accustom ourselves to being glad that there is no need to raise our voices in order to speak to Him, since His Majesty will make us conscious that He is there, we shall be able to say the Pater Noster (Our Father) and whatever other prayers we like with great peace of mind, and the Lord Himself will help us not to grow tired. Soon after we have begun to force ourselves to remain near the Lord, He shall give us indications by which we may

understand that, though we have had to say the
PaterNoster (Our Father) many times, he
heard us the first time. For he loves to save us
worry; and, even though we may take a whole
hour over saying it once, if we can realize that
we are with Him, and what it is we are asking
Him, and how willing He is, like any Father,
to grant it to us, and how He loves to be with
us, and comfort us, He has NO WISH TO TIRE
OUT OUR BRAINS BY A GREAT DEAL OF
TALKING...For love of the Lord, then sisters,
accustom yourselves to saying the PaterNoster
in this recollected way and before long you
will gain by doing so.[3]

As already pointed out, this is consistent with Christ's
own teaching on prayer. Keeping the point of your consideration simple is the formula for successful meditation
because its aim is vertical not horizontal. It's not for the
quick reading of the merits of many ideas but for the slow
savoring of the wisdom of one or two. So letting the single
seed of a thought impregnate the mind and heart so as to
affect outlook and behavior in a positive way may be a fair
definition of meditation.

Thus this less busy, non-discursive form of prayer all
Christians (or members of all the various faiths) could
practice with great profit, especially beginners in mental
prayer. It's an approach that avoids any taint of "Quietism"
because the mind is not totally passive, while, at the same
time, it is not so burdened with active thinking and interior
acts that, stuck on that level, it is unable to transcend. This
way, the garden gate to contemplation can easily swing open.

In truth, one should not be concerned about just being
idle during mental prayer, but for those who may be, the
above formula seems like a happy compromise between the

idea of doing nothing at all and doing too much. A simple concept is all that's necessary. For instance, just mentally repeating the phrase "Our Father", according to one's own spontaneously felt rhythm and pace, would be sufficient. There would be really no need to recite the whole thing since that one phrase suggests in itself (especially to those familiar with it) the whole meaning of the prayer.

Yet even if the Church should still find something "quietistic" about this recommendation, then each phrase of the prayer could still be mentally recited, slowly and easily, one by one. This would not provide any obstacle to transcending and one could take as long as one would want, even a whole hour, as St. Theresa suggests.

This approach is similar to St. Ignatius' method who wrote in his "Spiritual Exercises" - a book which has contributed so much to the religious life of people - the following:

> We may take, for instance, the Lord's prayer and start to recite it from the beginning, but stop at the very first phrase, 'Our Father'. This we make the basis of a meditation and stay with it as long as we find in it various depths of meaning, comparisons, interest or other development of a prayerful spirit in us. And this we do with a subsequent word or phrase of this or some other vocal prayer or liturgical formula.

> While using this mode of prayer, if it should happen that we spend the whole hour fruitfully on one or two words or phrases, we should postpone finishing the rest of it in this way for another time, and instead, at the end of the

hour merely recite the remainder of the prayer
in the usual way.[4]

If we read carefully what St.Ignatius is saying here,
we can conclude that he is emphasizing not only absolute
simplicity of subject matter but also spontaneity, that is,
permitting the mind to go in what ever direction it wants in
the slow and thoughtful recitation of the prayer.

Based on this reasoning, the Church would likely
approve of this method of meditation. So instead of
skimming over many ideas, or, even worse, just mouthing
vocal prayers in rote fashion, the meditator could consider
one or two simple but significant truths of his or her faith,
allowing them to sink in, quietly and effortlessly. This
Ignatian "relishing" of the thought, is both a correct form of
meditation as well as the correct mental posture for
contemplation since it calls for an easy, no-strain attitude
throughout the meditation.

This could well be called a contemplative kind of
meditation in which simultaneously the values of both modes
of prayer are achieved through a harmonious, working
relationship. But, at the pain of repetition, it may be wise to
respectfully suggest that Trappist Abbot Thomas Keating's
premise behind just having one thought in meditation may be
in error. He says that the purpose of just having one thought
is "to slow down the normal flow of thoughts."[5]

As already discussed, since they are an indication of
the release of stress within the nervous system, there is
nothing wrong with the flow of thoughts during meditation.
Any attempt to block them or any trying to force the mind to
be still, however gently, is counter-productive, a waste of
time and energy.

The same goes for Fr. Pennigton's counsel to "take a
minute or two to quiet down"[6] at the beginning of medi-

tation, as if there's something wrong with the mind not being quiet. He seems to be advocating making some effort to quiet the mind. Again, you don't try to quiet it down and there's nothing wrong with restlessness, as just explained. The mind, moreover, may not instantly favor you with quieting down within the first few minutes no matter what you do or don't do. But whatever it does, it's always for the good. The mind takes care of itself. Flowing thoughts, like a brook flowing into a pond, always seek their own serene level though in their own good time. This is the mind's natural tendency. So why not just let it be?

Indeed, this is an exercise of true faith in God and the mind which He created. Any trying, therefore, to manipulate or control during meditation is self-defeating because active effort is intrusive and tends to prevent the mind from transcending. "Unless you become as a little child..."

In addition, since no thought in contemplation is necessary in the first place, neither is a pious thought. However irreverent this may initially sound, it is, in fact, the exact opposite. By way of explanation, Fr. Pennington suggests that in meditation we take up a simple word like the name of Jesus "and begin to let it repeat itself within."[7] However beautiful the sentiment, this mental repetition of the Holy Name, such as the mental repetition of a mantra, has no efficacy in itself nor does it serve as a kind of holy intermediary to somehow bring about the desired effect since, as one's personal experience will prove, the same result is achieved when we make no mental effort whatsoever. Far from being irreligious, this premise simply implies that man's closeness to God is such that no words, however pious, are necessary to reach Him. You just knock and the door opens. In fact, there is no need even to knock. You just wait in the lobby.

So the point of having some simple thought during meditation is not to somehow improve things by controlling. Its use should be only a matter of personal preference such as for the comfort and encouragement you may receive of thinking of something pious or uplifting. But you can take the thought or leave it since comfort, deep relaxation and encouragement come anyway with or without a thought. But if you don't want to let go and prefer to hang onto something, then let the thought be simple and its mental repetition, effortless.

As for the mantra method, as made popular by Maharishi Mahesh Yogi, it is based on the supposition that some kind of thought such as a mantra, a meaningless, sanskrit sound, is needed for the mind to transcend. According to the Maharishi, the mantra is chosen by a trained expert in meditation on the basis that the vibrational quality of the sound must fit the vibrational quality of each individual and since each individual is different, each one gets a different sound. He explains:

> The influence of a spoken word that is carried by the waves of vibrations in the atmosphere does not depend upon the meaning of the word. (To interject: What? Meaning has no influence? Author) It lies in the quality of the vibrations that are set forth. Therefore, where it is necessary to produce vibrations of good quality that produce an influence of harmony and happiness, it is also necessary that the quality of vibration should correspond to that of the individual.

> Individuals differ in the quality of their vibrations which constitute their individual personalities. That is why the selection of a

proper thought for a particular individual is a
vital factor in the practice of transcendental
deep meditation.[8]

The fact is, however, that each meditation expert of
the Maharishi's is given a certain set of mantras to distribute,
about eighteen in number. They are assigned to the novice
meditator based on what age bracket he or she may be in.
One may wonder, then, what this standard of choice has to
do with vibrational match-ups.

The Maharishi's method works, however, but it has
little to do with the theory since the theory is, apparently, not
what it is proclaimed to be. The best guess as to why it
works is that this renowned teacher rightly emphasizes
effortlessness in the mental repetition of the mantra and that
it is just a simple, meaningless sound. In other words, this
method lays little or no burden on the mind. But if you
meditate and actually do nothing, as already stated on page
one, the same result is achieved. You will find that the mind
quickly moves on its own, with no mantra or word as a
vehicle, on the path to inner peace.

The reader, however, may want to make up his or her
own mind by experimenting either with the mantra or
without it, that is, if anyone wants to invest $400 to receive
one from the International Meditation Society, or the reader
could use Fr. Main's suggested mantra (maranatha) at no
cost at all. Before embarking upon this trip, however, one
may want to be reminded of the words of Christ: "When you
pray, do not multiply words." Would not this counsel not
also refer to the needless repetition of a mantra? Or recall
St. Theresa of Avila saying, "...though we have had to say
the Pater Noster (Our Father) many times, He heard us the
first time."

But, according to the Maharishi, the mantra is regarded as an indispensable and proper vehicle for the mind to transcend. Yet, at the same time, he teaches in his three day meditation course that it is dispensable because he advocates thinking the mantra not in a hard, focused, concentrated way. This means the meditator is advised to let the mantra go if it tends on its own to slip away from one's awareness. This apparently contradictory advice may explain why the Maharishi has had to set up an elaborate system for checking his clients' meditations to make sure meditators are maintaining the proper balance as they walk the high-wire of this subtle instruction.[9]

So all mantra or simple-thought methods contain this risk to the novice meditator: He or she may easily slip into focused concentration, the great imposter, because the individual is told the thought is indispensable to reach the ground floor of one's inner being. (It's like telling a person he can't touch his own nose without some outside help). But if you dispense with the simple thought or the mantra, then you have, literally, no problem. That's why it is wrong to tell people they can't meditate unless they have an instructor or guru to teach them (at great expense) when meditation is so ridiculously simple. By the way, is it possible to provide expert instructors for the entire world? Some instruction is necessary, of course, which is: just sit quietly and take it as it comes.

If this teaching seems quite dogmatic, it is no more so than those who propose the opposite view. The reader, however, has the choice of deciding for himself or herself which method seems better. The methodless method, proposed by this author, is based on a great respect for the human mind and the Creator which designed it. It is based on the fact that contemplation seems like an intuitive act, that is, no intervening medium or mantra crutch is required, just as normal eyes see light or normal ears hear sound, directly. It is based on the commonly held, religious belief that God is as close to each person as each person is to himself or herself, even closer. He supports every atom in our being. There can be no greater intimacy than that which exists between man and his Creator. As children we were taught that even the hairs on our head were numbered. That seemed quite astonishing to us when we first heard of it as it still must be to us now. Of course, if He is responsible for maintaining in existence every atom of our physical being, then the hair count is a cinch. More than that, as the story of the Prodigal Son teaches us, if our loving Father sees us from afar coming up the path, throwing aside all restraint, He runs up to embrace us with a kiss. These parables seem to imply that there are no barriers between the soul of Man and his Maker. So maybe there's no need to climb over them by some kind of technique such as mantra chanting or focusing on some thought.

But is the experience of transcendence the same as infused contemplation ? If we read St. Theresa's following account of what she called perfect (or infused) contemplation, we can see similarities: (The reader can judge for himself or herself whether the two are identical)

> .....I must tell you that, while you are repeating the PaterNoster (Our Father) or some other vocal prayer, it is quite possible for the Lord to grant you perfect contemplation. In this way His majesty shows that he is listening to the person who is addressing Him, and that, in His greatness, He is addressing her, BY SUSPENDING THE UNDERSTANDING, PUTTING A STOP TO ALL THOUGHT, AND AS WE

> SAY TAKING THE WORDS OUT OF HER
> MOUTH, SO THAT IF HE WISHES TO SPEAK
> SHE CANNOT DO SO, OR AT ANY RATE NOT
> WITHOUT GREAT DIFFICULTY.[10]

Also:

> The faculties rejoice without knowing how
> they rejoice; the soul is enkindled in love
> without understanding how it loves...

> It is well aware that this is not a joy which can
> be attained by the understanding....

> This, daughters, is perfect contemplation.[11]

If there is any difference between the "supernatural" gift of infused contemplation and the spontaneous experience of transcendence, it seems difficult to understand from the above quotation what that difference is. Again, this is not meant to be a denial or an affirmation of Church doctrine, only an observation.

According to Church doctrine, however, there need not be any confrontation between what is "natural" and "supernatural." She teaches that the supernatural builds on and enhances man's natural state in a harmonious, cooperative relationship, that Man must do all that he can, as far as he is able in his limited capacity, using all his faculties, to achieve his salvation. In this way, he cooperates with God's grace. Yet without "supernatural" support, the Church also teaches, he will not be successful. In effect, she is saying that people must do all that they can, in a natural way, to help themselves, and, at the same time, realize their absolute dependence on God's help as well. God helps those who help themselves.

Therefore, since the ability to transcend is another natural function of the mind, certainly it should be utilized in the name of spiritual progress, just like any other mental power. But if theologians of the Church insist that contemplation is purely a supernatural gift, this is their belief. No useful purpose is served in disputing it. The fact, however, that the mind's ability to transcend is as natural as its ability to reason cannot be denied. It may not be supernatural, but it's a fact of life which can be proved to any doubting Thomas who, by just sitting quietly for a few moments, is open-minded enough to believe his own experience. Should not then this natural ability of the mind be used to good advantage from the very beginning of the "spiritual journey"? It could be regarded as a prelude to, not a substitute for, its supernatural counterpart, the so-called "gift of infused contemplation", which is supposed to be granted, according to traditional teaching, only after a long period of spiritual purification.

Therefore, it would seem to be a mistake for a spiritual counselor to advise clients not to engage in this natural form of contemplation in the mistaken belief they must go through the "purgative way" before moving onto contemplation. Why should the one have to precede the other? Transcending can be a powerful component and ally of the purification process. Rather, would it not be wiser to heed the teachings of Saints Ignatius and Theresa who have shown the need for simplicity in prayer even for beginning meditators, a formula which happens to fit the requirements of successful contemplation whether you consider it to be natural or supernatural, infused or innate?

So even for a novice, if he or she feels the spontaneous need during meditation not to be mentally active but simply to be in peace, it should not be regarded as laziness or a waste of time, as St. John made clear:

> They should (meditators) allow the soul to remain in rest and quietude, even though it may seem very obvious to them that they are doing nothing and wasting time, and even though they think this disinclination to think about anything is due to laxity. Through patience and perseverance in prayer, they will be doing a great deal without activity on their part. All that is required of them here is freedom of soul, that they liberate themselves from the impediment and fatigue of ideas and thoughts and care not about thinking and meditating. They must be content simply with a loving and peaceful attentiveness to God, and live without the concern, without the effort, and without the desire to taste or feel Him. (Author's interjection: Why is it assumed this would be difficult?) All these desires disquiet the soul and distract it from the PEACEFUL, QUIET AND SWEET IDLENESS of the contemplation which is being communicated to it.[12]

This experience of blissful quietness could last the whole meditation or come only intermittently, but to avoid the alleged pitfalls of "Quietism", the meditator can just easily return to the point of consideration as soon as he becomes aware that he has wandered off or transcended. Actually, and this is true more so for beginners, this contemplative kind of meditation is usually an experience of four random events: 1) the experience of transcendence, 2) the experience of the mind wandering, 3) the experience of the mind effortlessly considering the point of the meditation, or 4) the experience of transcending simultaneously with some degree of mental activity, either of the mind wandering or considering the point(s) of the meditation. You can never tell from one meditation to the next which of the four possibilities will predominate. All you can do, as St.John suggests, is not interfere.

Sometimes the feeling of transcendent peace or ecstasy, could happily persist throughout the entire meditation. At other times, restlessness and mind-wandering could prevail. But whatever happens, all one can do is take it as it comes, a point which, even at the risk of repetition, cannot be emphasized enough.

Therefore, a certain amount of patience and detachment is needed to go along with this uncertainty of never knowing ahead of time what the experience will be. But these are virtues which the meditation itself tends to foster even though, ironically, it is itself the reason for needing them. This detachment, then, requires that the meditator not try to manipulate the meditation in any way to reach a more desirable result. Of course, it is only human to prefer consolation over restlessness but the irony is that meditation is not governed by the laws of cause and effect. In fact, any attempt on the meditator's part to bring about some effect actually inhibits the effect. The effect occurs only when we do nothing to make it occur which means that in meditation the law of cause and effect operates in reverse. This doesn't mean, of course, that we are helpless. A beneficial result is always achieved except that we don't have to do anything to achieve it.

So in one sense, we have no control over what happens in meditation; yet, in another, we do because we can always open the door. But it opens not because we push but because we just sit and wait. It's the same attitude, really, that we have - or should have - before going to sleep. We don't need to make any effort to go to sleep. This would be counter-productive. We need only to lie down and wait for it to come or maybe do some light reading and drift off. It's not an unfamiliar posture. The difference, however, between sleep and meditation is that sleep sometimes is fickle. Sometimes it's late in coming or does not come at all but meditation never fails us. The mind can easily transcend or move quickly to clear the path of any stresses that may temporarily block the way. We don't even have to knock and the door opens.

This principle of detachment, however, should be not taken too far. It should not mean that novice meditators be required to suppress a reasonable hope for attaining the goal of transcending in each meditation and, eventually, the goal of enlightenment. No. This is the Zen concept of detachment which asserts that since enlightenment is a state of perfect freedom or detachment, then to attach oneself to the goal of enlightenment is to practice the exact opposite of what the goal means. Therefore, to hope for the reward of enlightenment is only to guarantee that it never will be reached.

The logic behind this seems elegant but sometimes logic has a way of leaping over reality and falling on its face. If you try to take normal motivations away from people, if you require enlightened behavior from them prematurely, it's the same as asking the boy to play the man. Before gaining that spiritual maturity and level of detachment which is characteristic of enlightenment, people have no choice but to function on the level of maturity where they happen to be at the moment. If they are asked to breathe at too high an altitude, they will collapse in due time from sheer exhaustion, overcome by discouragement and self-hatred because they know, if they are honest with themselves, they cannot maintain that level of detachment asked of them, nor pretend to be indifferent to the goal without losing sight of it altogether.

But since the regular practice of meditation is an absolute necessity for the attainment of the goal, a normal person needs motivation to keep at it. He needs the stimulus of seeing the light at the end of the tunnel. It's only when he reaches the light (of enlightenment), that this high level of spiritual detachment becomes authentically genuine, not contrived or forced through self-delusion.

There are also other ways by which this principle of detachment can be misinterpreted to an extreme. One kind of extreme, for instance, is the advice commonly given by certain spiritual advisors concerning "sensible consolations" according to which meditators are advised not to be attached to them, hope for them or rest in them should they occur during meditation. It is based on the caution that the meditator not confuse the means with the end, that is, to confuse the pleasure of meditation with its more substantial goals.

But there is a certain consolation in meditation which is inherent to the nature of transcendence just as mountain air cannot smell anything but sweet. The suggestion, therefore, seems absurd that the meditator should try to detach himself from this pleasant feeling or to feel somewhat guilty because he or she may be enjoying the meditation. We have a natural right to enjoy the peace and consolation whose fragrance naturally breathes from the experience. We should be encouraged by this feeling and not be made to feel guilty over it, rather to patiently expect that this gift of transcendent joy become a permanent part of our lives.

Perhaps, then, it would be better advice for the novice to accept the sweetness of consolation when it comes but not to be discouraged when it is overshadowed by the forces of stress-release and inner healing because only good can come out of either experience. Putting it in a religious context, if the feeling of God's presence in the soul is comforting, is this not how it should be? Or is there supposed to be a distinction between the feeling of God's presence within the soul and God Himself? If there is, then how can one know that God is present? How can one be told to love the wine but be indifferent to the taste? This is the kind of reasoning which is the basis of Puritanism.

Of course, if by "sensible consolations" the advisor is referring to visions, revelations, spiritual messages, voices and so forth, then the advice is good. The purpose of meditation is not to have visions and the like. If they occur, they may or may not have some meaning in themselves, but they have no meaning for the more sublime purposes of meditation. It is best to regard them as interesting experiences and let them pass. To give them any importance beyond that or to act impulsively upon them would indeed be unwise.

Just as one, therefore, should not have to act "detached" in order to meditate successfully, neither is a high degree of virtue, as is commonly taught in religious circles, a prerequisite. For that matter, no virtue at all is required except whatever it may take for one to begin meditating in the first place. The ability to transcend in meditation is a natural ability and is not the result or the reward of a more virtuous or religious life; rather, the reverse is true. Virtue is the result or the reward of meditation. Meditation then is the means for attaining enlightenment not the result of enlightenment.

The same reasoning obtains for "infused contemplation" (whether we assume that transcendence and infused contemplation are the same or not). Why is it taught that the gift of infused contemplation is granted only after an arduous journey up the spiritual path? Is it not more logical that if God is a loving Father, as many religions teach, that He would be just as solicitous for the beginner in the spiritual life as for the advanced, and that his loving embrace (experienced in infused contemplation) would be given from the very beginning when devoted seekers need Him the most, not withheld until they are considered virtuous enough to approach Him? Yet this is the traditional teaching of the Catholic Church down through the centuries. St. John of the Cross best expresses this point of view in the following excerpt from his commentaries:

> First let him (the beginner) have an habitual desire to imitate Christ in everything that he does, conforming himself to His life: upon which life he must meditate, so that he may know how to imitate it, and to behave in all things as Christ would behave.[13]

St. John then is, in effect, suggesting an absurdity, namely, that one must be enlightened in order to be enlightened. This is not to imply that one shouldn't strive for virtue, enlightened or not, but to ask a beginner in the spiritual life to be like Christ is obviously asking the devoted seeker to begin at the end. The advice is unrealistic. Sainthood is not achieved overnight. If St. John, however, is only pointing to this as a laudable goal, then this would make more sense but such a high-level of sanctity should not be regarded as a prerequisite to contemplation. This is like putting the cart before the horse.

Some may note another contradiction in the Church's teaching which is that man must earn or "predispose himself" for this supernatural gift despite the fact that a gift, by definition, is not earned; it is freely given. And who is qualified to say when supposedly it has been? The only way one can know if he or she has the ability to contemplate is to try it out. How can we know what our abilities or "gifts" are unless we unwrap them and find out? It makes no sense to counsel people not to try to contemplate based on the presumption that they would only be deluding themselves. The inner peace of transcendence is a clear and unmistakable experience which should not be denied people simply because some misguided counselor discouraged it.

But if the beginner is advised to meditate only discursively, he will more likely follow the advice, not daring to presume that he could have experiences like the advanced. He will then try to keep his mind busy, in some way, throughout the meditation with pious reflections and interior acts, thereby keeping his mind effectively sealed off from the greater benefit and joy of contemplation. Yet in this activist approach, is not the Church disregarding the good counsel of Christ Himself who recommended that we should not multiply words during prayer? Presumably, he meant as well the multiplication of ideas and interior acts since all these involve the same kind of loquacity of which he disapproved. His good counsel should be heeded. As for more detailed study and considerations of Church doctrine, the time for that would be in spiritual readings, sermons, discursive meditation, catechetical instruction, the liturgy of the Mass and so forth. If the Church wants people to pattern their lives after Christ's example, then let them be properly instructed in His simple method of prayer, as echoed in the teachings of the great doctors of the Church. The Church, therefore, seems to make prayer a difficult task, if she advocates St. John's more discursive approach in meditation. Moreover, he perceives God as a distant deity who will not come to his children in a more direct way unless they are first purged of all their imperfections.

This grindstone theology, however, that emphasizes man's spiritual weakness and sinfulness in his natural state, does not give due credit to God's generosity, at least, as Christ would have us understand it. Man's ultimate happiness rests, according to the Church, in beatific union with his God, but he has not been given any innate ability to reach Him. So he is like a bird destined to fly but without wings. But would God, the loving Father of the New Testament, create Man for Himself and then make it, or allow it to be, difficult for him to reach His outstretched arms? Although the story of the Prodigal Son was briefly referred to earlier, it seems appropriate here to quote this most moving excerpt from the text:

> But, while he was still along way off, his father saw him, and took pity on him; running up, he threw his arms around his neck and kissed him. (Luke 15, 20-21).

The same point is made in Luke:

> Among yourselves, if a father is asked by his son for bread, will he give him a stone? Or for a fish will he give him a snake instead of a fish? Or if he is asked for an egg, will he give him a scorpion? Why then if you, evil as you are, know well enough how to give your children what is good for them, is not your Father much more ready to give from heaven, his Holy Spirit to those who ask him? (Luke 11, 11-14)

Christ said also, "The Kingdom of God is within you," a statement seconded by Muhammad and quite consistent with Sankara's frequently quoted words that the Self is Brahman (the Self is God). This is an unconditional statement which seems to contradict St. John's more ascetical concept that God won't come to you (directly in contemplation) until you first clean up your spiritual house. Furthermore, to make the gap between creature and creator even wider, the Church has, down through the centuries to this day, espoused and sanctioned the so-called Dark-Night thesis of St. John which essentially says that God is light, but man, in his fallen state, is darkness, and that the spiritual path toward divine union is necessarily painful. He writes:

> Yet a doubt arises: Why if it is a divine light (for it illumines and purges a person of his ignorance), does the soul call it a dark night? In answer to this, there are two reasons why this divine wisdom is not only night and darkness for the soul, but also affliction and torment. First, because of the height of the divine wisdom which exceeds the capacity of the soul. Second, because of the soul's baseness and impurity; and on this account, it is painful, afflictive, and also dark for the soul. 14

St. John also compares man to the owl, blinded by the light of God:

> The brighter the light, the more the owl is blinded; and the more one looks at the brilliant sun, the more the sun darkens the faculty of sight, deprives it and overwhelms it in its weakness. 15

Then there is the greatest darkness of all, the dark night of despair which, ironically, is supposed to come to those who are far advanced in the spiritual life. Again, St. John:

> Thus, although a person suffering this purgation knows that he loves God and that he would give a thousand lives for Him....He finds no relief. This knowledge rather causes him deeper affliction. For in loving God so intensely that nothing else gives him concern, and aware of his own misery, he is unable to believe that God loves him. He believes that he neither has nor ever will have within himself anything deserving of God's love, but rather reason for being abhorred not only by God but by every creature forever. He grieves to see within himself reasons for meriting rejection by Him Whom he loves and longs for.[16]

Furthermore, he cannot be persuaded otherwise even by his spiritual director who "... may point out many reasons for (his) being comforted on account of the blessings contained in these afflictions..."[17]

Since this state of despair is apparently beyond remedy, then one wonders what good it does to warn people of this black cloud if they aren't going to benefit by the warning anyway. But how can the Church reconcile this doctrine of despair and dark-night thesis with her constant admonition that we should at all times be joyful in the Lord? Does not the Church also teach that despair is a sin against the Holy Spirit? Therefore, it seems hardly possible or believable that the contemplative way could result in such a nightmare as described by St.John.

Though we have been blessed with many important reflections of the Saint concerning man's spiritual journey, the blessings have not been unmixed. He lacks consistency as well as the leveling rigor of the scientific method. His sweeping generalizations and compelling style are replete with Biblical quotes but strangely oblivious of the need for factual documentation. Intrinsic contradictions abound in much of his teaching, which would take another chapter of this book to point out, while his dark-night theory comes to us without even one concrete example from among his contemporaries who may have suffered this spiritual agony. We have, therefore, no obligation to assume without some kind of credible evidence that man's religious pilgrimage is necessarily painful and dreary, especially since contemplation, the vehicle of the "God experience", if you regard it as such, is a natural ability of the mind, or if supernatural, a gift, if God is good, He'd swiftly bestow.

It is surprising, then, that four centuries later, there seems to be no change in the Church's thinking toward St.John, as popularized in the brochure by Fr. Venard Polusney, entitled "Attaining Spiritual Maturity for Contemplation" (according to St.John of the Cross). The pamphlet is simply a rehash of the traditional teaching of St. John that the contemplative way must be preceded by the asceticism and dark night of the purgative way. As Fr. Polusney writes:

> The way of the beginner is ascetical, that is, he strives to acquire perfection by his own efforts, assisted by ordinary grace: he is the predominantly active agent. When he enters the illuminative way, or the contemplative state, he begins to enter the mystical state: that is, God becomes the more active agent in perfecting the person, and the person becomes the recipient, especially in his prayer life.[18]

It would be better, perhaps, if the pamphlet were entitled, "Attaining Spiritual Maturity THROUGH contemplation and the Purgative Way." Theologians, queasy about this idea, could be reminded of the natural ability of the mind to transcend, as has been discussed. The joy and strength of contemplation, in its natural mode, (at least, if you accept this distinction between natural and supernatural) should not be put off until some later time if it's already at our immediate disposal. The purgative and the illuminative way should go hand in hand with the contemplative mode of prayer, serving as a powerful ally of spiritual growth and purification, not a separate path in itself.

Obviously, there are growing pains in the spiritual life which are intrinsic to any maturation or learning process, but this is far cry from the despairing depths of which St. John speaks. Each time we meditate there is necessarily involved a certain amount of contrast or conflict in the experience. When the mind dives within and enjoys serene transcendence, the deep peace and joy of this is in sharp contrast to the more shallow and confusing experience of daily life. So, after each meditation, the novice meditator may sense a certain sense of loss because that inner depth of serenity cannot be fully maintained in the normal, waking state, though in time it will be. But it would be inappropriate to label this mild distress as a dark night of the soul, unless you enjoy indulging in sixteenth-century-Spain, religious rhetoric.

Those who meditate for long periods of time, say, in a retreat or as a matter of daily practice, could experience greater discomfort of dryness and irritability owing to heavy-stress release brought on by the long meditations. Add to this the fact that long meditations dramatically lower the metabolic rate, making it somewhat stressful for one to keep pace with the normal demands of life, unless, of course, if one is on retreat, and there are no demands. But this discomfiture could hardly be likened to the agonies of hell. Meanwhile, as common sense would seem to dictate, the cure for the above-mentioned afflictions is through the avoidance of excessively long meditations as a daily practice. All things in moderation. If the meditator maintains a sensible balance between his meditation time and his daily activity, there should be no problem, as already discussed in "Practical Hints."

A careful reader of St. John's works could end up wondering if the "Doctor of Doctors" even took his own teaching seriously. After indulging in dark-night metaphors and hyperboles in the first part of his book, you find him further on trying to soften the blow, so to speak, of his forceful language by greatly moderating or amending his words, even to the point of frequently contradicting himself. For instance, he writes in the following paragraph of the "delightful effects" of the dark night after having earlier referred to it as an agony.

> Through this inflaming of love we can understand some of the delightful effects of this dark night of contemplation now gradually produces in the soul. Sometimes, as we said, it illumines in the midst of these darknesses, and the light shines in the darkness. (Jn. 1:15), serenely communicating this mystical knowledge to the intellect and leaving the will in dryness, that is, without the actual union of love. The serenity is so delicate and delightful to the feeling of the soul that it is ineffable. This experience of God is felt now in one way and now in another.[19]

In yet another passage, he continues to contradict himself when he speaks of the so-called agony of the spirit as a very healthy state of mind, in fact, one which approximates the final goal of religious life, divine union.

> The soul consequently arrives at the true fulfillment of the first commandment which, neither disdaining anything human nor excluding it from this love, states: "You shall love your God with your whole heart and with your whole mind and with your whole soul and with all your strength." (Dt. 6:5) This love is now beginning to possess something of union with God and thereby shares to a certain extent in its properties.[20]

This picture of a man deeply in love with his God and "neither disdaining anything human nor excluding it from this love" is not the picture of any unhappy person in a dark night of despair. He is, in fact, describing the state of enlightenment, the perfection of disinterested love. The dark night, therefore, judging from the above excerpt, now seems like a very encouraging and hopeful state. It seems too bad, then, that St. John's love of imagery, which led him to perhaps overwork the metaphor of light and darkness throughout his writings, has led to so much contradiction and confusion.

St. John, of course, is correct in emphasizing the need for detachment in the spiritual life but perhaps incorrect in insisting that deprivation, in any sense of the word, has some necessary relationship to holiness. Otherwise, we would be forced to conclude that the slums of the world are the fertile soil of sanctity - which is, of course, hardly the case. We would also be forced to conclude that wealthy men, by and large, are spiritually doomed. Christ, of course, never said that prosperity, of itself, is an obstacle to salvation. He was referring to those who "put their trust in wealth." If wealth itself were a problem, then the Church would have no logical reason to denounce the social injustice of poverty and none at all for holding onto its Vatican treasures. Of course, this is not meant to imply approval of the crazed pursuit of excessive wealth.

But one's financial condition, contrary, of course, to traditional belief, has no inescapable effect on one's spiritual life. Saints as well as sinners have emerged from the ghettos of the poor as well as from the mansions of the wealthy which, in turn, proves that spiritual detachment is a matter of interior disposition, not actual deprivation. A poor man can be as greedy in his poverty as a wealthy man in his abundance. Monks, who take a vow of poverty, are not necessarily detached because they are poor (though they are told actual poverty helps toward that end), but because their interior life is sufficiently enriched, hopefully, as to make poverty or wealth in their lives a matter of profound indifference. Their life of contemplation produces an inner exaltation and happiness which, of itself, gradually and automatically fosters the appropriate detachment required of them.

The idea, however, that one can effect this interior disposition simply by assuming its outward appearance flies in the face of common sense and experience. Detachment is borne of an enlightened state of bliss-consciousness which makes self-evident the fact that true happiness does not depend on the shifting winds and circumstances of life.

This inner detachment, however, does not rest on stoical indifference. Life is like a wedding banquet. It's there to be enjoyed...the food, the wine and the music but not just for themselves. As invited guests, our enjoyment of the feast must rest on the more fundamental joy of the wedding, the happiness we share with the bride and groom. But if the bride or the groom (or both) don't show up, the guests cannot truly enjoy the celebration. It's this higher purpose that fosters the proper sense of detachment. So true detachment is based, not on deprivation, but on a higher Good. When a person possesses that deeper joy which radiates from within, he automatically puts all the pleasures of life in their rightful, subordinate place. If we understand, therefore, that detachment is simply a question of a proper perspective, it then becomes irrelevant to suggest, if an individual gives up all right to the ownership of material goods or the right to a normal sex-life, that he has thereby found some kind of a short-cut to enlightenment.

Similarly, the rationale for the theological premise that married couples with children and a home in which to raise them are somehow not as close to God as poor celibates may need some re-examination. It seems like a profoundly contradictory kind of theology that would suggest that man's sexuality and normal desires for marriage, a home and the customary possessions of married life are not as conducive to spiritual perfection as the life of the celibate. If religion teaches that God created man's instincts and that he can know his creator indirectly through the wonders of his creation, then why would the joy of a normal, loving family-life, an important and wonderful part of that same creation, not lead to the same appreciation of His love as any other part?

The creature comforts of life do not in themselves draw us away from God. It's ignorance, the ignorance of not knowing how to reach Him in contemplation, which, in turn, leads to confusing the tree for the forest, the merely relative for the Essential, and expecting from a wonderful, though fleeting world, what it cannot give: that transcendent fullness

of happiness which can only be achieved, spiritually, through
the regular practice of contemplation.

NOTES

CHAPTER 1

1. Raymond Van Over, "Eastern Mysticism", *Selections from the Writings of Sankaracharya* (New York: New American Library, 1977), p. 159.

2. (Phaedo, 79c)

3. Lawrence LeShan, *How to Meditate* (New York: Bantam Books, 1974), p.14.

4. Maharishi Mahesh Yogi on the Bhagavad Gita, *A New Translation and Commentary* (Baltimore: Penguin Books, 1969), p.314.

5. Ibid., p.314.

6. Thomas Merton, *Love and Living* (New York: Farrar, Straus and Giroux, 1979), p.41.

CHAPTER 2

1. *Satapatha-Brahmana*, (10.6, 3, 1-2).

CHAPTER 3

1. Katsuki Sekida, *Zen Training* (Weatherhill, Inc., N.Y. 1975), p.46.

2. Ibid., p. 31

3. *The Collected Works of St. John of the Cross*, Kavanaugh and Rodriguez, Translators (Washington D.C., ICS Publications, 1973), P.285. Original reference: *The Ascent of Mt. Carmel*, Book III, Chapter 42, 1.

4. Ibid. Original reference: *The Ascent of Mt. Carmel*, Book III, Chapter 42, 2.

5. R. K. Wallace and H. Benson, "The Physiology of Meditiation", *Scientific American*, Vol 226, No. 2, Feb 1972, pp. 84-90.

6. P. W. Corey, *Airway Conductance and Oxygen Consumption in Human Subjects via a Wakeful Hypometabolic Technique*, National Jewish Hospital, Denver, Colorado, April 1973.

CHAPTER 5

1. *The Collected Works of St. John of the Cross*, Kavanaugh and Rodriguez, Translators, (ICS Publications, Washington D.C., 1973), p. 149. A translation of an excerpt from *The Ascent of Mt. Carmel*, Book II, Chapter 15, 5.

2. Ibid. p. 152. A translation of an excerpt from *The Ascent of Mt. Carmel*, Book II, Chapter 16, 10.

CHAPTER 6

1. St. Theresa of Avila, *Interior Castle*, Fourth Mansion, Ch. iii, 6.

2. *St.John of the Cross, Complete Works* (trans. by E.A.Peers, Newman Press, Westminister, Md., 1957) Vol.3, 159, n.32).

3. St. Theresa of Avila, *The Way of Perfection* (A Double Day Image Book, New York, 1964), pp. 193-194.

4. *Spiritual Exercises of St.Ignatius Loyola* as translated by Fr. Lewis Delmage, S.J. (Wagner, Publisher, New York, 1968) P.128.

5. Thomas Keating, "Cultivating the Centering Prayer", *Review For Religious*, 36 (1977), p.11.

6. M. Basil Pennington, "Centering Prayer—Prayer of Quiet", *Review for Religious*, 36 (1976), p.657.

7. Ibid.

8. Maharishi Mahesh Yogi, *Transcendental Meditation* (New York: The New American Library, 1963), p.51.

9.   The following are the instructions given by teachers of Maharishi Mahesh Yogi to meditation initiates on how to use the mantra:

> Mental repetition (of the mantra) is not a clear pronunciation. It's a faint idea and if at any time you seem to be forgetting the mantra, don't try to hold on. Let it go. Take it as it comes.

Here the Maharishi emphasizes the secondary role of the mantra in meditation because the meditator is told not to maintain a firm grip on it but be willing to give way to other forces as when the mind tends to wander and the meditator accordingly forgets the mantra or when, having transcended, the mind wants to be quiet.

So what is happening if the mantra's role seems so secondary? Is it playing any causative or facilitating role at all in the mind's operations during meditation or is it just a dispensable bystander? How can anything be proved one way or the other when, it seems, the same effects occur without the mantra? Or to counter the argument that the meditation would be more effective with the mantra than without, how can you prove the same effects would not occur to the same degree and extent when you don't use the mantra as when you use it? It seems impossible to prove one way or the other. You'd have to be able to use and not use the mantra at the same time in order to compare the effects but this is impossible.

So what is the point of the mantra? What role does it play? Why is it considered indispensable on the one hand but you can forget about it on the other? What proof has been brought to show that it is a necessary or facilitating vehicle for the mind to transcend, or what evidence adduced, beyond unproved, interesting assumptions, to show that its use has any significance whatsoever when, if you don't use it, the same results occur?

10. St. Theresa of Avila, *The Way of Perfection*, translated and edited by E. Allison Peers (A Double Day Image Book, New York, 1964), p. 170.

11. Ibid. p. 171.

12. *Collected Works of St. John of the Cross*, translators Kavanaugh and Rodriguez, O.C.D. ICS Publications, Washington, D.C., 1973, p. 317). A translation of an excerpt from *The Dark Night*, Book I, Chapter 10, 4.

13. *St. John of the Cross, Complete Works* (Sheed and Ward, N.Y. 1953) Vol 1, 57, n.3)

14. *Collected Works of St. John of the Cross*, translators Kavanaugh and Rodriguez, O.C.D. ICS Publications, Washington, D.C., 1973, p. 335. A translation of an excerpt from *The Dark Night*, Book II, Chapter 5, 2.

15. Ibid. p. 335. A translation of an excerpt from *The Dark Night*, Book II, Chapter 5, 3.

16. Ibid. p. 343. A translation of an excerpt from *The Dark Night*, Book II, Chapter 7, 7.

17. Ibid. p. 341. A translation of an excerpt from *The* Dark Night, Book II, Chapter 7, 3.

18. *Attaining Spiritual Maturity for Contemplation* (Living Flame Press, N.Y. 1973) P.8.

19. *Collected Works of St. John of the Cross*, translators Kavanaugh and Rodriguez, O.C.D. ICS Publications, Washington, D.C., 1973, p. 357). A translation of an excerpt from *The Dark Night*, Book II, Chapter 13, 1.

20. Ibid. p.353. A translation of an excerpt from *The Dark Night*, Book II, Chapter 11, 4.

BOOKS AND ARTICLES
QUOTED OR REFERRED TO IN THE TEXT

Ignatius of Loyola, St: *Spiritual Exercises of St.Ignatius of Loyola* as translated by Fr. Lewis Delmage, S.J. (Wagner, Publisher, New York, 1968).

John of the Cross, St: *The Collected Works of St. John of the Cross*, Kieran Kavanaugh, OCD, and Otilio Rodriguez, OCD, Translators (Washington D.C., ICS Publications, 1973).

John of the Cross, St: *St.John of the Cross, Complete Works*, translated by E.A. Peers (Newman Press, Westminister, Md., 1957).

P. W. Corey: *Airway Conductance and Oxygen Consumption in Human Subjects via a Wakeful Hypometabolic Technique*, National Jewish Hospital, Denver, Colorado, April 1973.

Lawrence LeShan, Dr: *How to Meditate* (New York: Bantam Books, 1974).

Thomas Merton: *Love and Living* (New York: Farrar, Straus and Giroux, 1979).

Katsuki Sekida: *Zen Training* (Weatherhill, Inc., N.Y. 1975).

Theresa of Avila, St: *The Way of Perfection* (A Double Day Image Book, New York, 1964).

Theresa of Avila, St: *Interior Castle*, translated by E. Allison Peers (Doubleday, New York, 1964).

Raymond Van Over: "Eastern Mysticism", *Selections from the Writings of Sankaracharya* (New York: New American Library, 1977).

Venard Polusney, Fr: *Attaining Spiritual Maturity for Contemplation* (Living Flame Press, N.Y. 1973, a pamphlet).

R. K. Wallace and H. Benson: "The Physiology of Meditiation", *Scientific American*, Vol 226, No. 2, Feb 1972, pp. 84-90.

Maharishi Mahesh Yogi: *Maharishi Mahesh Yogi on the Bhagavad Gita, A New Translation*, (The New American Library, New York, 1963, a Signet Book)

Maharish Mahesh Yogi: *Transcendental Meditation* (The New American Library, New York, 1963, a Signet Book).